"The Cape was a country of its own,
with its own geography,
its own history, its own languages
and culture.
In this mythical Cape
the Coloured people were rooted,
and, to a lesser extent, the Afrikaners too,
but Africans were aliens, latecomers,
as were the English."

— J. M. Coetzee, *Summertime: Scenes from Provincial Life*.

A LONG ROAD

PREFACE
///////

Thinking of South Africa, our contemporaries remember the image of Nelson Mandela leaving the Victor Verster prison on 11 February 1990 at eleven in the morning. The head of the black rebellion had spent twenty-seven years and one hundred and ninety days in jail. The whole world is watching this man who, in his elegant suit, holds his country and Africa as a whole in the hollow of his hand. One expects a revolutionary but then he bends over to a little white girl and takes her in his arms. He holds her against his heart and gives her a kiss. Mandela, who suffered so much, is a man of peace!

The country of apartheid, torn by ancient hatreds, is taken by this simple yet difficult gesture, that of forgiveness. South Africans and the world are moved by this grace, this kiss. The aura of Mandela becomes universal, hundreds of millions of people begin to dream of a new fraternity, of a reconciled and more just world.

Until his death in 2013 Mandela did not change; he told us that when one does not betray his or her dream of dignity and freedom, it pierces hearts: "No one is born hating another person because of the colour of his skin, or his background, or his religion," he wrote. "People must learn to hate, and if they can learn to hate, they can be taught to love, for love comes more naturally to the human heart than its opposite."[1]

Build, construct, repair and pacify society: that is the moral legacy of Madiba, Mandela's affectionate nickname in South Africa. The task is arduous, thankless, daunting, and we can understand nothing of the remarkable work of architect Carin Smuts presented in this book if we do not understand, at least in outline, what history and what culture she comes from. Or rather, she returns to.

To be called Carin Smuts in South Africa, is like being a Churchill in Britain or an Eisenhower in the United States. It is being part of the historical legend of the country.

Jan Smuts (1870–1950), Boer general, Marshal of the British Empire, South African Minister of Defence, Mines, Interior, Indigenous Affairs, and Justice before becoming prime minister twice, was one of the founders of the League of Nations in 1920 and the UN in 1945 for which he wrote the preamble to the Charter.

This statesman, whose ancestors were French Huguenots and Dutch (Afrikaner or Boers), was born in the days of British control over this land of farmers, the "white tribe" of Dutch, German and French—all Protestant—peasants who had conquered their farms from the Zulu tribes in fierce battles. The discovery of fantastic gold and diamond mines awoke London's interest in these colonies. In two wars the Afrikaners were crushed. Around 1900 the English invented the concentration camp for them, killing twenty-eight thousand women and children of the Boer fighters by famine.

Jan Smuts is one of several distinguished Afrikaners who helped the

1
Nelson Mandela, *Long Walk to Freedom*. London: Little, Brown and Company, 1994.

*"He longed for the day when everyone
in South Africa would call themselves nothing,
neither African nor European
nor white nor black nor anything else,
when family histories would have become
so tangled and intermixed that people
would be ethnically indistinguishable,
that is to say—I utter that tainted word again—
Coloured. He called that
the Brazilian future."*

— J. M. Coetzee, *Summertime: Scenes from Provincial Life*

Anglophones establish the young South Africa after 1910. This did not withhold the ambitious character from accompanying the political revenge of his countrymen who, militarily defeated and economically crushed by the Anglophones would, thanks to their birth, gain political power in forty years time.

The era of racial segregation started in 1877 (the principle of white superiority and establishment of indigenous reserves, Colour Bar). At the time of British colonization, it continued to strengthen and Jan Smuts actively contributed to it. For the operation of their gold mines, the British wanted black labour to replace the Afrikaner whites who were paid four times as much. The claims of the small Afrikaner whites and those of the Communist Party (with the slogan "Workers of all countries, unite for a white South Africa") were smothered in blood by Jan Smuts, prime minister in March 1922.

The global crisis of 1929 would further radicalize the Afrikaners. Pastors in these rather crude and often destitute communities played the role of intellectuals, forging a protective ideology of their community based on the belief that they were different from others, a "chosen people". After the Second World War, when the Afrikaners became the majority, the Calvinist creed of predestination and an interpretation of the curse of Noah against his son Ham (reputedly black and deemed to be cursed and enslaved forever and ever) would lead to the establishment of this great heresy of Protestantism: the policy of apartheid, meaning "apartness".

Individuals were classified into four groups (whites, blacks, Indians and Métis) determining their habitats, their marriages, their education… in short, the coexistence of groups that never live together. The purpose of this policy was to ensure that the Boers, having become a minority relative to blacks, enjoyed maximum protection against other ethnic minorities. This policy, initially tolerated by Americans and other Westerners (as it was fiercely anticommunist), ended up costing a too-high price. Sanctions were imposed and even prevented the Afrikaners participating in international rugby tournaments, which was important there.

In the late 1980s the South African army had only one ally left, Israel. Not having air supremacy, it suffered a defeat against the Cubans in Angola. Domestically, South Africa found itself in the situation of France at the end of the war in Algeria: the control over townships led the country to a standstill. The army and the South African secret services twisted the politicians' arms and prepared to release Mandela. In his cell, he could receive whomever he wanted to rediscover the reality of his country; they offered him the whole world's press.

Carin Smuts drew her strength from her granduncle and Mandela. She planted her roots in cultures and lands she did not know, she listened,

listened for days and months, she invented an architecture at the same time joyful, economic, different, and for people who were perfect strangers to her and became friends. These black populations for which she envisioned a different urbanism.

Live together, build, pacify
and rebuild South Africa.
I give you Carin Smuts.

Good reading!

François Hauter[2]

2
François Hauter is a French journalist and novelist, winner of the Albert Londres Prize for his coverage of events in South Africa.

ANATOMY
CS STUDIO

OF A DREAM

CONTENTS //////

DIALOGUE OF FASHION AND DEATH. ON FORM IN ARCHITECTURE, TRANSCENDING NECESSITIES

/////////

On the occasion of a workshop for architecture students, I saw and heard Carin Smuts express her annoyance at a young student's question about the relationship of the forms of her building with those of Frank Gehry's universe. She refused to discuss the idea of a formal affiliation, clearly blocking the invocation of visual references that would outline the character of a line, a style. It would first of all have been the submission of the forms produced by CS Studio Architects to a sense of anticipation, as understood in art history in the age of *Stilgeschichte*,[2] and then convoke them against their will onto the global stage of spectacle that architecture has become. I will use this interaction to address a fundamental question that arises in the contemporary international context. The built environment, more generally the constructed environment, has in recent decades positioned itself as the centrepiece of a planetary spectacle. This show is contradictory, paradoxical, cumulative, dramatic, fascinating, and always producing strong images. On the right of this universal stage, we find the field of ruins from Kabul to Tripoli where the "ones" conduct wars to annihilate all tangible signs of the existence of objectionable civilizations, while "others" attempt to monopolize mineral resources and anticipate lucrative reconstruction contracts. The gigantic production capacity that the "others" control, especially in the domains of construction and arms, suggest the complementarity of the interests of the "ones" and the "others".

On the left of the stage the picture is hardly less violent. Often presented as inevitable, everywhere metropolization advances at the expense of the natural environment. To say that the results are not convincing is an understatement. Think of the disaster of the artificial "islands" in Dubai. The sandbanks behave very differently than the engineers' models and require extensive maintenance with dredging and sand supply to withstand the ocean's forces. The large emerging metropolises are built in a dramatic context of spatial segregation, based on exploitation of the construction proletariat. Think of the slaughter of the workers who were literally enslaved on the sites of the Doha stadiums. These phenomena are characteristic of the field in which the unbridled competition of "urban marketing" takes place, governing the construction of the worldwide "Brandscape".[3] The arena in which time and again the extravaganza of technology and form is displayed, invented by what communications firms, for reasons of necessary semantic interference call "architecture agencies", is a place of extraordinary violence. In architectural terms, the result is of repulsive vulgarity. All that said, placed side by side these extravagances show "same, same, but different". The question is how this context affects individuals, architects, and engineers, and what can really become of the "free will" of those "creators" and the determinism they are subject to.

1
See p. 96.

2
This paradigm enabled art history to make "allocations" based on stylistic characteristics and their evolution. It is the basis of the Belser Stilgeschichte, a famous German collection that begins with the volume *Frühe Hochkulturen, Aegypten, Mesopotamien, Aegaeis* (1969) and ends with *XX. Jahrhundert and Konfrontationen* (1971). The now rather dated enterprise covers Europe and the ancient Middle East, and endeavours to present the image of a continuous progress of art.

3
A neologism formed by the contraction of "brand" and "landscape", designating the landscape created by trademarks.

At the time of exacerbated individualism, the architect's ego tends to play a disproportionate role and to focus attention on a category that is supposedly "their creative thinking" being all of a sudden "liberated". In Spinoza's famous letter to Schüller,[4] he presents a solid and intelligible basis for thinking about the problem of this freedom: "I call free, for my own part, something that is and acts by the sole necessity of its nature; whereas constraint is determined by another to exist and to act in a certain definite way." Architecture is clearly of the second category. That of CS Studio Architects conceives and asserts itself as determined by the actual conditions of life in South Africa, especially by the lives of black people, starting before the collapse of the apartheid regime. It belongs so strongly to the second category that it corresponds, as we will see, with a very clear cultural and social project in the spirit of CS Studio Architects. It stems from commitment. CS Studio Architects builds, primarily, in order to respond to the needs of people and communities, many of which have been excluded in the past, notably from the architectural order. It has in nothing to do with the self-referring scene of images circulating at the speed of light. This global stage, on which so many "stars" and pretenders believe they must profile themselves, is first and foremost dependent on economic and ideological mechanisms, the dark side of the force, wielding the "invisible hand" of Fashion. Spinoza knew similar situations. They led him to say: "Such is human freedom that all boast of possessing her whereas it only exists in those men who are conscious of their appetites and ignore the causes that impel them."[5] Georg Simmel spoke of connecting with a "source"[6] to rely on: "The gain for which we fight is not given by nature but by man ... One who proposes should seek to constantly spark new needs, ever more original, in whom he is paying court."[7] In short, this could be the karma of stars. It is with this quote that an Italian sociologist[8] introduced the argument that "[metropolises] liberate forms from their dialectic with nature, and thus from the character of sacredness, of necessity, of utility, while embodying a playful dimension of thought, and therefore growing, multiplying, stratifying, and differentiating or even better breed under the influence of desire". The metropolis would be the place par excellence in which a self-referential world would make objects, artefacts, both ends and means, a "device" "on which historical life is based and unfolds". Against all odds, the problem is that for social reasons the issue of natural resources and their limited availability in a finite world cannot be ignored. The described "device", which even made sustainable technology a fashionable phenomenon, simply participates in the unbridled flight into frantic of our technical, fetishist, proliferative species, whose habitat in recent decades is indeed named Metropolis. The problematic

4
Spinoza, "Lettre à Schuller", in *Œuvres*, Paris: Garnier-Flammarion, 1995, vol. 1, 303-304.

5
Ibid.

6
Concept developed by Augustin Berque, "Séminaire 'Questions de mésologie'", Mésologiques: http://ecoumene.blogspot.ch/2011/01/prises-et-de-prises-berque-catastrophes.html.

7
Georg Simmel, *Philosophie de la modernité*, vol. 1, trans. Jean-Louis Vieillard-Baron, Paris: Payot, 1989, 248.

8
Antonio Rafele, "La Mode et la Mort. Réflexion sur W. Benjamin" in *Sociétés*, no 97, 2008.

assembly allowing the growth of this kind of optimistic metropolitan ideology is of a basic simplicity. It requires, as in a retraction operation, that the fundamental question, the only one actually deserving of reflection, of humanity's relationship with nature be abandoned. Since it has become difficult to deny, it is declared resolved, falling under a past that for the occasion is called "Malthusian" and substituted in a manner of which the superfluous turns have proven effects on the majority of individuals. Roman power was based on "bread and circuses" whereas contemporary authority is based on the fetishism of commodities and technology, with fashion dictating its rhythm. Fashion is the big deal; this mechanism is well established above the principles that are supposed to govern our life in society. It laughs at the separation of powers, human rights, protection of data and privacy; it presides over our destinies, treats them and mistreats them without a single moment of worry about the price of its undisputed reign. The most naive believe it to be a recent phenomenon, hoping that society will secrete antibodies that ultimately will prevail. It seems that the matter is as old as the spread of the market society. There are witnesses! In 1824, in his *Dialogue of Fashion and Death*,[9] Giacomo Leopardi highlighted the obvious superiority of the former over the latter. Fashion, addressing Death: "I was saying that by nature and by our action we have in common that we continually renew the world. You, from the beginning you're taking up with people and life while I content myself with touching beards, hair, clothes, furniture, architecture, and so on... More generally, I compel the finest people to daily endure a thousand fatigues and thousand inconveniences, often as many pains and suffering, and I sometimes even push some to choose, out of love for me, a glorious death... Moreover, I have established such rules and manners in society that life itself, as for the body as well as the soul, is more dead than alive." The great illusion is to believe that designers and architects have the keys to a better, more adequate, attractive form. Those who participate in the style of Fashion never doubt their legitimacy; it is not in their DNA. In contrast the founding partners of CS Studio Architects, Carin Smuts and Urs Schmid, are deeply devoted in their practice of architecture to a dialectic of forms with nature, necessity and usefulness. They have a clearly Vitruvian DNA, making them assign form to the category of "beauty". In this sense, the forms found in their architecture can communicate with all those that are known, and carried out all the more freely because usefulness and consistency (*firmitas*) free them from Fashion. The Vitruvian system has no theoretical significance;[10] it simply looks very much like writings on art and in this context the three terms *firmitas*, *utilitas* and *venustas* are the vertices of the triangle of architectural affairs. A building outside that realm must necessarily have

9
"Dialogue de la Mode et de la Mort", in *Petites œuvres morales*, 1824, trans. Joël Gayraud, Paris: Allia, 1992, 24 and 26.

10
This claim contradicts authoritative discourse, especially the excellent *Vitruve et le vitruvianisme, introduction à l'histoire de la théorie architecturale* by Georg Germann, (Lausanne: PPUR, 1991).

transgressed one of the three basic criteria and can be called an extravagance.[11]. This is essential and it is fascinating to see how for example a global agency like Herzog & de Meuron attempts to bring it into disrepute. For them "the ancient trilogy… is obsolete… and suitable only as case for historians or the mayor's speech at the inauguration of a new museum or a chapel."[12] So that after a long and contradictory account,[13] in which the architects begin by convening around an alpine vernacular masterpiece, state its *firmitas* literally absolute, of a different order, perfect and therefore impossible to match, and then neutralize the concept on the grounds of the unavoidable complexity of the world, before disqualifying it altogether. This attempt to ideological production is understandable. As sophisticated and vain as it is, it does not seem less essential to its authors; it probably confirms their own level of uncertainty and is essential to asserting their authority in the production of ideology.

A clear view of this context and a deep understanding of the mechanisms at play are the kernel of Carin's response to her visitor's question. If a certain idea of form haunts the work of CS Studio Architects, it remains subject to the dialectic discussed by Simmel. Next to Carin, the young interlocutor seemed well brainwashed and just landed from the frenzied world of the global box office of fancy forms. He provided the viewer an opportunity to try and decipher the lines of code underlying this case.

"But let's go into the created things that are all determined by external causes…"[14]

Speaking of architecture that attracts her attention, Carin Smuts gladly cites Michael Graves, whose method she holds dearer than his work, and does not fail to speak of her interest in Frank Gehry's methods, while Urs Schmid calls for an approach that relates to Ralph Erskine. It is possible to see a contradiction when mentioning these architectural worlds even if they are not condensed to their formal appearance and far from that. The thing is not contradictory as long as we focus on the perceived appearance of form. In the spirit of CS Studio Architects it is obviously the idea itself by which architecture can be reduced to mere formal cohesion, perceived sequences, and technical or programmatic constraints, that is rejected. To CS Studio Architects it is of course obvious that architecture has a face, a look, and is subject to be shown. The problem is in fact as old as the image[15] and fits into the use that is made of it. The response to the student simply said: In architecture, the forms finally obtained do not mean much in themselves and do not speak beyond themselves. They interact with the look of the observers that question them. In sum, Carin said: Your question, inspired by the world of education dominated by proponents of cultural marketing, only tries to identify and place our architecture in the global register of

11
The *Dictionnaire historique de la langue française* as well as *Littré* reduce this term to a Latin etymology: *vagary*, meaning "keep out of the way, wander". An architecture that is outside the triangle of qualities mentioned by Vitruvius will therefore be either unstable, unfit for use, or deliberately ugly. The way of naming things as chosen by Vitruvius comes down to formulating the conditions by which what is architecture and what is not is determined. To give this idea both flexibility and strength, we must remember that the shape of the triangle has a latitude for variation. Its angles are not necessary equal.

12
Recently in a box on their website, next to nothing less than a conceptual masterplan for the Universal Exhibition in Milan, proposed in 2009: https://www.herzogdemeuron.com/index/practice/writings/essays/firmitas-de.html.

13
Reworked version of Jacques Herzog's lecture at the ETH Zürich, October 1996.

14
Spinoza, "Lettre à Schüller".

15
Yves Bottineau-Fuchs, *L'Équerre et le Pinceau, L'architecture dans le tableau, IXe-XXe siècle*, Arles: Actes Sud, 2013.

ready-to-wear brands: therefore it is out of place. After a literally perverse contemporary inversion, today it is the image of the thing that monopolizes attention and not the thing itself. Now I, architect, if I do not ignore anything of the inevitable image of the thing that I build, I invite you specifically to abandon the iconological field of representation and casual associations, and I invite you to consider that thing in cohesion with the processes that gave birth to it. It shows human beings, busy designing and building a shelter for their cultural activities, in the womb of a particular community.

What remains once these mediologic[16] elements have been defined is to pick up the pieces according to the constraints that fragmented them and attempt to explain how the images that architects convey nevertheless appear. The point is to try and understand this interest in Graves, Erskine and Gehry, and their relationship with the constructed thing perceived pars pro toto as an image. It is on the one hand to elucidate how the field of architectural design is structured and effectively organized, this phase in which forms, colours and the behaviour of light evolve; where functions are harmonized. On the other hand it is about how structures, use and construction fit together. For it is this complex reality made of the actions and emotions of its actors that is virtually held hostage by the short circuits of the metadiscourse of formal interpretation. Curiosity or concerns about equity would in principle urge one to try to grasp how the reception of architecture comes into being especially in schools, how the visual propaganda of the global Brandscape keeps on its message, washing brains and replacing the authentic architectural culture with a world of labile forms that it invites students to join. Where yesterday we trained architects, we now claim we stimulate their creativity. The full exercise, for which we lack room here, would allow to paint a picture by means of collage and juxtaposition, of the literally tragic misunderstanding at the origin of the evoked scene. Anyway, all these elements will be divided into words and sentences of critical discourse, become part of a currency and thus subject to exchange, hoarding, inflation and, as such, devaluation. Adjectives, language elements and references are markers of ideologies. The multiplication of their occurrence depreciates and degrades them and eventually triggers indifference, submission and even rejection! It turns out that what one might call a "key to happiness" is on closer examination a "fetish of decline".[17] The rebellious spirit is recognized by the fine perception of the used vocabulary; it knows the relevance of the way things are named. In other words, CS Studio Architects is in nothing driven by fashion and its overpowering phenomena delivering to a frenetic 24/7 market, 365 days a year, or the necessary "innovations" for archi-

From left to right:
Alain Uyttebrouck, Carin Smuts
and Urs Schmid.

16
Régis Debray,
Cours de médiologie générale,
Paris: Gallimard, 1991.

17
These terms are borrowed from Walter Benjamin, *Œuvres, II*, Paris: Gallimard, 2000, p. 215, quoted by Enzo Traverso in the preface to Daniel Bensaid, *Walter Benjamin, sentinelle messianique*, Paris: Les Prairies Ordinaires, 2010.

CARIN SMUTS

tects and their clients, or the busy burning of our world's finite resources on all sides. Fashion feeds on two sources: the past and amnesia. It plunders the first in a frenzied dance that summons forms already seen and having served, for recycling in a world it cannot see but "post-modern", and following modernity in architecture, reduces the past to a style. The second, amnesia, is maintained by the show's own noise. However, nothing is more stubborn to fashion than an observer gifted with memory.

Referring to Odysseus, Jean-Luc Godard in *Le Mépris* brings the Villa Malaparte back to its bare origins: a cave on the sea, topped by the cape on which Odysseus throws "the first look ... when he sees his country"; the director took care to put this replica in the mouth of Fritz Lang, known to have studied architecture, and by doing so en passant blows off the fragrance of modernity with which critics like to incense the villa, recalling that Odysseus gave up immortality for Ithaca.

CS Studio Architects has developed a practice focusing on attention to the culture of the client and end users. This "listening" is part of a highly interactive integrated process that especially transfers effective power to users and whenever possible even on the construction site. In every project, every situation requires the implementation of a dedicated and original process, making it a tool that works in all phases of its development. The goal is to really transfer decision-making authority to users and leave it to the architect to create forms out of the collectively taken decisions. In order to work perfectly, the process must be linked to a practice that affords shared competences. Integration of users in the process of construction releases the energy of human groups, facilitates their appropriation of the created spaces, and ensures sustainability. It gives them the only truly worthwhile characteristic and the only bulwark against obsolescence, that of identification with the built thing. In this process, the architects come down from their egoistic pulpit and abandon the idea of authority based on technical or administrative control or coming from the idea of "the project" or "good form"; they renounce their prerogatives. "By listening to people, the architects are provided with a wealth of information to feed into the design process. In the process of participation, role-players are empowered and they take ownership of their design decisions."[18] The architect's talent will manifest itself in its ability to deliver a compelling work in this particular field and the specific information and constraints it generates.

The architect remains the one who will ensure the stability of the structure, its functional performance, and the synthesis of light, shapes and colours. It takes place in an environment diametrically

18 "Our Philosophy", CS Studio Architects, http://csstudio.co.za/Philosophy.html.

opposed to that of "participatory processes", CS Studio Architects: "Participation is generally seen only as a social process. This is when it fails."[19]

19
Ibid.

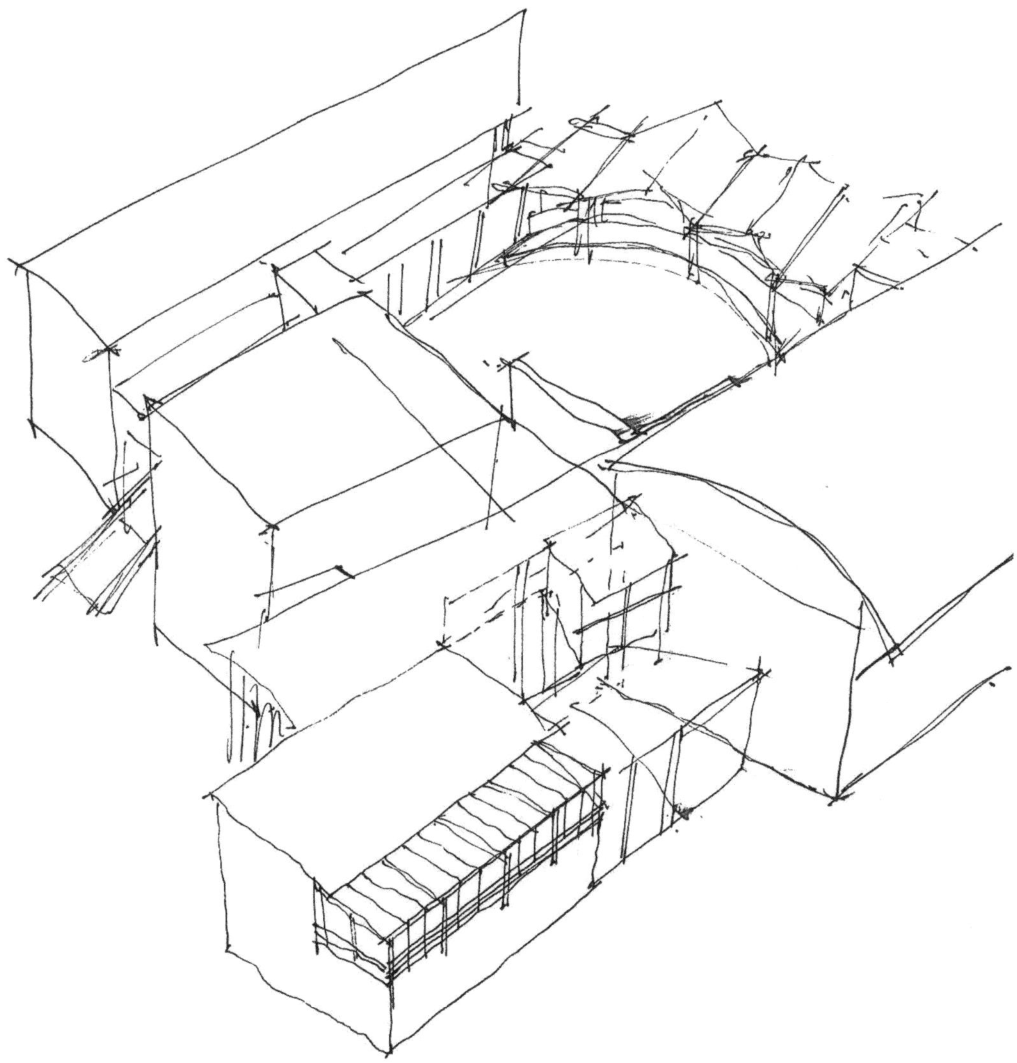

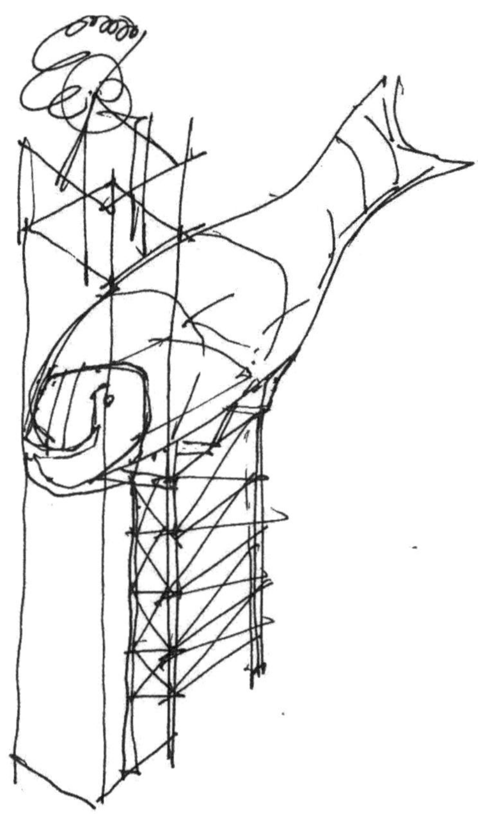

HOW TO WATCH WHALES IN HERMANUS BAY?

PROJECT, PLAN, VERIFY, COMMUNICATE

/////////

The famous site of Cape Province[1] obviously allows tourist to set sail on a motorboat for a marine mammal safari and thus, one suspects, disrupt the whales' lives. On the coast however, a rocky lookout cape and a didgeridoo player calling cetaceans would suffice to enjoy an exciting show. By its orientation and location, the view brings one to meditate on the virtual prism that, between the human eye and the observed, determines our perception, our understanding. The observer can drift away on thoughts about not only the chosen frame as in the Renaissance, but also about the ancient astronomer who inferred from the shadow of a stick planted in the sand that the earth is a sphere and even calculated its circumference with admirable precision.

Art history in the twentieth century focused on the symbolic character of perspective in the Renaissance,[2] related with a philosophy of space. This resulted in an exaggerated emphasis on perspective. I will come back to this later. The primitive hunter with his bow and arrows probably nourished himself with symbols, but he and his children ate the product of the hunt. And that depended on the accuracy of his shot, controlled by his eye, his brain and his arms. Similarly, the architect, the client, the user of the built object and the workers on the site cannot escape from the relentless rule of reality, not even for a moment. They are left to their visions, their tastes, and their time. They undergo the intensive bombardment with images that all kinds of actors carry out on them. They become subordinate to an ideology transcribed in images. Fashion and architecture magazines, urban planning regulations, building materials dealers and financial institutions all weigh on the imagination of customers as well as on that of other players in construction. They lay down the preconceived images, pretended to be the product of free will.

Technical tools for design and architectural representation do not operate neutrally in this context. It is the aim of mediology, a discipline that emerged in the early 1990s, to propose an approach to overcome this opposition of technology and culture. It studies the material basis of ideologies and beliefs, and the effects of technical innovations. This is the actual stake of our argument here. "In some community sites we exchange ideas with users weekly often more than two years before picking up the pencil."[3] There is no better way than by this patient caution that we can express the idea that the architect is aware of their prescriptive power, the authoritative status of their technical instruments and that they are concerned not to impose them on users and on clients. This delicate approach is obviously based on the consciousness of their position as *transfugitive*.[4] As an Afrikaner assimilated into the English elite, or as Swiss associated with that society, Carin Smuts and Urs Schmid come from the white world, the world of power, but they left the key of both

1
"The Southern Right Whale", hermanus.co.za, http://www.hermanus.co.za/whales.

2
Erwin Panofsky, *Perspective as Symbolic Form*, trans. Christopher S. Wood, New York: Zone, (1927) 1991.

the prerogatives of their corporation and the senseless academic favours of the "participatory approach", to engage on the ground, to take sides, and clearly answer the old question: "Which side are you on?"[5] From a mediological point of view, this principle choice has obvious implications that materialize in the requirements of functionality and the management of documents produced by the architects. This is an essential condition if we want the project to not only express the will, expectations and beliefs of users, but to also incorporate the added value of the architect's art while subjecting the whole to the actual and continuous control of the users. The talent and skill of the architects consists of translating these needs without betraying them. The faithful and loyal transcription is achieved through the implementation of effective tools for design and communication, understood by all and in which all can interfere. In this view, as is understood intuitively, the scale model is an essential instrument.

Representation: the stubborn resistance of reality

Alberti, who published a book entitled *De Pictura* in 1436,[6] tried in his *De Re Aedificatoria*, written from 1442 and printed in 1485, to identify the particular characteristics of architectural representation in order to distinguish the art of illusion, number and proportion. Early in the second book he treats, from a point of view focused on the economy of the material, the means of control that the architects have at their disposal before building. The scale model appears before anything else as a pre-paratory stage of construction, but it also serves to complete the design. Moreover, it is regarded as an object of independent study.

New information technologies are fascinating because they allow remote control of flying machines, and load them with arms and ammunition. However, they have done little else than model, codify and duplicate the generalized perceptions and actions of the prehistoric archer.

All prostheses merely extend the scope and speed up the impact of human incursions on the environment. They do not change the basic conditions in any way. This is obviously true in architecture, although with a considerable difference: if the market demands from new information technologies a spectrum of very specific features meant to accelerate a number of secondary processes that occur in the technical office, it generally comes no further than rather primitive representations. In twenty years of architecture modelling, the average quality has altogether remained quite summary. Despite its limitations, the model is essential to the vast majority of design operations because of its precision, its reproducibility to infinity, and the gains in productivity it brings. Whereas the rigour and power of calculation have always been imperatively required

3
Carin Smuts in an interview with the author, Western Cape, September 2014.

4
From the Latin *transfugere*, "cross over to the enemy".

5
A song written during the 1931 miner's strike in Harlan County, Kentucky, sung to the tune of a traditional Baptist hymn, it was recorded by many artists, including Pete Seeger.

6
http://laperspective.canalblog.com/archives/2009/02/13/12518073.html

for the development of architectural projects, the mode of representation, often called "simulation", invites itself almost for free and therefore primitive "above the market". Synthetic visualization was initially offered to the designer but, like a Trojan horse, allowed software makers to place their mode of virtual representation in the foreground through the images seen by planners, policy makers, customers, users and authorities. Through this breach it has flooded the world. The distant sight of the whale leaping out of the sea is now substituted with the simulation of the sea, the whale, the cape, and some amazing algorithms to know the depth, salinity and water temperature, instead of going time and again to the sea itself, the whale or God the father. In architecture this general misunderstanding results in the urge to build what was displayed on the screen. "What you see is what you get", the computer manufacturer said, and next planners worked the alliteration of that slogan to: "What you get is what you see [on the screen]." This mechanism has plunged us into a world where the story of the child taken to the countryside by his grandmother, discovering cows and asking, "Where's the remote?" has become plausible. That is to say, a world where the ease with which it is possible to substitute on a screen one image by another, change its colour, texture and perspective, eventually leads to an altered, neutralized and literally indifferent perception of actually built architecture. The right technical resources available today allow everyone to "see" what they want to see and to record in the memory of their camera nothing but the image filtered by the chosen settings. If I want to remember the Jin Mao Tower, I could photograph it under a fluorescent yellow pixel checkerboard but would inevitably end up believing and saying it is its real appearance.

An Amish use of models

The only problem with all this technical stuff is that it conceals the spray, the iodine smell of the ocean, the fatigue, the urge to pee, and the emotions and interaction of people among each other. All the things that characterize life in society, of which it is certain that today it has completely degenerated into a science-fiction caricature. Engineers have repeatedly promised that the next update will solve all these "details". In fact, new features will be introduced, the price reduced with the future obsolescence of the product in mind, creating new needs, and not addressing its insurmountable disadvantages. It is noted here that the question of presentation of architecture for design, communication and implementation is trapped in a loop following technological developments since the nineteenth century. Successive innovations like watercolour drawing, tracing paper, gravure prints, photography, CAD, CAM, etc., continue to produce the same effects; through the accumulation of tricks they create distance between designers, builders and users. It is certain that technological advances have accelerated and accentuated this successive dispossession, this alienation of the protagonists regarding the building project. The latest IT developments, catalogues with objects based on product catalogues, reach to the ultimate goal: to implement the prescription to consume such goods and services in the architectural design process.

The conservative lamentation over this state of affairs and this trend is not my point. Frugality is not to turn away from the evolution of technologies and to deprive oneself of the productivity benefits they provide. Various authors argue, probably rightly, how humans and their technologies co-evolve. In a chapter on the rapport between American Amish communities and technology in *What Technology Wants*,[7] Kevin Kelly notes that no major innovation has ever been permanently blocked by a ban, embargo or boycott. He highlights how the Amish bishops succeed, by subtle adjustments, to declare a kind of moratoria or waiting periods in the adoption of these technologies. In doing so they allow their parishes to develop a real culture of their use. They gain a certain benefit as they are less exposed to drainage of capital imposed by rapid turnover due to obsolescence, and that could be the reason why in crises these communities have shown to be more resilient than others.

This detour allows us to say that, in general, architects and planners have thrown themselves carelessly at new technology, and by doing so have engaged in a mode of production that tends to dispossess them of the fundamental instruments of their art. The verb, the drawing, the line in the sand, the mimed gesture and the model are vital instruments providing architects mastery of their ideas and intentions. They also offer them tools for communication and cultural action in their relationship with customers, with users. All these means, considered primitive, unproductive or superseded, are nevertheless likely to ensure the symbiosis between people and what they build.[8] CS Studio Architects is equipped with modern technology as it is available today, but the agency has maintained and developed its own methods for project development and communication. They correspond exactly to the nature of their architecture, which would be impossible without them. In its own way, CS Studio Architects makes a kind of Amish use of technology, in which the scale model plays a central role.

Once the architect has set priorities, such as focusing on the use of local materials and optimizing the expenditure of resources on wages for the local labour force, the adverse effects of the technological pyramid are deployed in a quite embarrassing "martingale".[9] If, on top of that, it is about offering people a vocational training during the course of a project or meeting the needs of a deprived

7
Kevin Kelly, *What Technology Wants*, New York: Penguin Books, 2010.

8
This theme was brilliantly developed in a doctoral thesis recently defended at the Swiss Federal Institute of Technology EPFL in Lausanne: Sytse de Maat, "On the Symbiosis of People and Building: The Perfect Slum", thesis 6459, EPFL, 2015.

9
The term "martingale" is a more or less scientific combination, intended to ensure the gains.

community, marginalized like black women in the townships of apartheid,[10] we understand that using state-of-the-art modern technology is not only inappropriate, but also perfectly counterproductive.

I do not know if Field Marshal Jan Smuts, Carin's granduncle, had the opportunity to see Queen Mary's Doll House,[11] the model designed by architect Edwin Lutyens, assisted by 650 leading artisans, at the same time when he was struggling with the gigantic project of the government buildings in New Delhi. Carin saw the model and grasped the depth this field of representation provides to immediate, complete and synesthetic perception, as it excels in implying, suggesting, confusing and distorting that perception. No one should enter the profession of architect without being confronted with this lesson that has no equal. For CS Studio Architects the scale model is a design and planning tool, while in its "community construction sites" in particular, the agency assigns contractual value to it. The model materializes the interaction with the users; it allows them to recognize the expression of their demand in the project. The model is in fact the security, almost the fetish of the occult contract by which architects engage themselves alongside the users, answering the only question that matters: "Which side are you on?"

10
https://en.wikipedia.org/wiki/Township_(South_Africa).

11
The model was completed in 1924 and seen by 1,617,556 people in the British Empire Exhibition at Wembley.

PUBLIC, SHARED, INTERSTITIAL AND NEGLECTED SPACES

/////////

In an already-old book *Le Seuil franchi*,[1] anthropologist Roderick Lawrence attracted the attention of generations of European architects, above all regarding the importance of transitional spaces, semi-public traffic areas that structure the in-between; from the street to the door, from public space to private space. They organize socialization by arranging passage, distance or proximity. They lay down the reach of sight, absorb noise, change the horizon of sound and make the space fit, allowing people to adjust attitude and manner in the transition between the busy and generally perceived hostile street, and the home with its own levels of intimate sphere. The recent European VERSUS project,[2] whose remarkable results were published in 2014, devoted an entire chapter to what the authors call "collective and shared spaces". Review of anthropological literature shows the importance of all spatial provisions that, by the uses they afford, are conducive to social cohesion, informal exchange and tolerance. It highlights the vital importance of these complementary spaces. In vernacular environments, these shared collective spaces generally have a flexible configuration, fragmented or modular, allowing variety in appropriation and constant renewal, and reflecting the plurality of lifestyles and diversity of societies. Finally, the study found that the analysis of vernacular environments allows us to perceive an implicit dimension of collective spaces, where informal processes of humanization continuously develop.

To say that in the field of architecture and urbanism of the twentieth century—dominated by the prescriptive eugenic and totalitarian visions of Le Corbusier's *Plan Voisin*[3]—this dimension was out of favour, is an understatement. In the second half of the century, when all were busy with rebuilding after the war in Europe and Asia (and mimetic developments in the rest of the world) the Californian teachings by architect and anthropologist Christopher Alexander were heard by a small minority and it took no less than twenty years before the magnum opus of his oeuvre was completed and readily available (1980–2002).[4] The recent interest of young researchers offers him a second life. The doctoral thesis of Dutch architect Sytse de Maat[5] contains case studies focusing on terrains already well known, but on which he has collected original data. One terrain is the "slum" of Dharavi in Mumbai. "Slum" is obviously a very crude term for this high density urban environment (between 800,000 and one million inhabitants on 223 hectares in 2007), which generates a considerable share of the India's GDP, partly achieved in export, and builds and rebuilds itself through investments which, while they obviously have nothing to do with the amounts involved in real estate development, are as least as impressive. Essentially, the information synthesized by Sytse de Maat identifies and extensively recognizes the creative properties of architecture without architects and especially

1
Roderick Lawrence, *Le Seuil franchi*, Geneva: Georg, 1986.

2
Mariana Correia, Letizia Dipasquale and Saverio Merra (eds), *VERSUS: Heritage for Tomorrow. Vernacular Knowledge for Sustainable Architecture*, Florence: Firenze University Press, 2014.

3
Review by the author of the book by Xavier de Jarcy, *Le Corbusier, un fascisme français*, Albin Michel, Paris, 2015 in *Tracés*, September 2015.

4
Christopher Alexander, *The Nature of Order: An Essay on the Art of Building and the Nature of the Universe*, Berkeley: Center for Environmental Structure, 2002.

5
This theme was brilliantly developed in a doctoral thesis recently defended at the Swiss Federal Institute of Technology EPFL in Lausanne: Sytse de Maat, "On the Symbiosis of People and Building: The Perfect Slum", thesis 6459, EPFL, 2015.

those of urban planning without planners. The important thing in this situation is the subsequent observation according which the vernacular practices involve countless adjustments between actors and that they result, within a careful economy of means, in an astounding social optimization and impressive properties of use and liveability of the city. An interesting indicator of these qualities came to me by the remark of a Dharavi resident to whom Sytse said we intended to take a train the next day to visit a rural area where many Dharavians come from. Our interlocutor responded with a firm, "Be careful, such areas are not safe!" He thus demonstrated that an "appropriated" space is a space in which its users, its creators, feel safe.

Such mechanisms of space appropriation are visible well beyond the field of architecture and urbanism. They are reflected in literature, comics, and film. Asked about this, an alumnus of Christopher Alexander, the architect and film director Amos Gitai[6] recognizes them as underlying some of his documentaries like *Wadi Ten Years Later*[7] and *House*,[8] and it is possible to see their manifestation in some of his fictions. Seen in this light, *Ana Arabia*[9] is not only a narrative film and a rare gesture: a single clip of 84 minutes, it is above all a stroll in the intermediate spaces of a neighbourhood. The film and narration cling to the common areas, a small square, a garden, a flight of stairs and a dwelling, where the thoughts and emotions of the characters emerge and crystallize. These spaces, by their residual nature and their configuration, literally forge the plot and precipitate the fragments of which they are the wings. The rigorous discipline required by the clip gives emphasis to the transitions. When the camera enters a room, the technical skill of the cameraman ritualizes the crossing of the threshold and increases the narrative intensity. The story of the spatial context suggests as well the lives that take place as those that are supposed to have been lived there. In Gitai's film, this is where the main character, a young Jewish woman, survivor of the death camps and immigrant to Palestine, has converted to Islam to share the love and life of a Palestinian Arab. The central figure is absent from the picture, but she literally inhabits the spaces, as articulated in empty and full, providing the perfect backdrop of scenes they allow to be called to mind, while interviewed witnesses are gathering their memories there. The difficult form of a single clip makes sense in the work of this architect making films, in so far that it gives the viewer the impression of unity of time and place, materialized in the fractal space that folds and unfolds before his eyes. The cinematic feat affords ideas to embody in the story and emotions to occupy the space that supposedly allowed them to hatch. If cinema is a play of shadows on the walls of the cave, this film can be understood as projecting them to the outside, in the interstices.

Amos Gitai, model for the film *Ana Arabia*, detail.

6
Amos Gitai graduated in architecture at Berkeley, where he subsequently took his doctoral degree. Interview with the author, 10 July 2015.

7
Documentary, 1991. http://www.amosgitai.com/html/film.asp?docid=39&lang=0.

8
Documentary, 1980. http://www.amosgitai.com/html/film.asp?docid=36&lang=0.

9
Fiction, 2013. http://www.amosgitai.com/html/film.asp?docid=84&lang=0.

Amos Gitai, location scouting for the film *Ana Arabia*, detail.

Life is fractal in nature

Niels Fabian Helge von Koch's[10] ideas on islands and the fractal length of coasts were invoked in debates on the relevance of the Darwinian hypothesis of evolution, because their supporters consider the fractal length of exchange surfaces, rather than the geological time scale and the timing of the manifestation of life on earth, likely to make Darwin's hypothesis plausible. Not so much because evolution lasted just as long as the progress of life would take, but rather because the exchange surfaces were practically of endless length. In other words, in the Darwinian hypothesis, evolution would not have had enough time if we would only consider its duration and not include the infinite fractal surface on which it took place. Similarly, the "holds" offered by architectural and *a fortiori* urban spaces, allow life to maximize its opportunities for interaction and to thrive in diversity. If we follow this logic, we must admit that speed, the straight line and smooth surfaces so paradigmatic of modernity according to Marinetti and Le Corbusier, offer even less "hold" on life whereas these characteristics are emphasized and rigorously implemented. In contrast, such areas offer even more control over space and what takes place there. It may be added by way of hypothesis that they stimulate the aggressiveness of those who face it, drawing the stage of the general class war that characterizes the globalized world.[11]

Various monographs on urban development direct our attention in the same direction. They are useful as demonstration, but obviously provide neither representative samples nor means of scientific proof; they simply reflect a phenomenon I consider of particular importance. In *Hong Kong In Between*,[12] two young architects methodically analyse the mechanisms of appropriation of tiny urban interstices, temporarily kept away from the hyper-policed attention of municipal authorities. Starting from the premise that the extreme density and the dizzying height of buildings in Hong Kong have preserved vast green spaces nearby while the public transport system has drastically reduced the role of the car (7 cars per 1,000 inhabitants, against 776 per 1,000 in the US), Borio and Wüthrich are interested in spontaneous uses, at the fringes of legal status and ownership, of "urban canyons" in which they observe with entomologist-like meticulousness, the use, appropriation and functioning. People seize those "holds" and establish working and living spaces. With much empathy, the authors present a lovers dictionary of forms of colonization, propose the thoroughly thought-through open-source project and present the prototype of a unique urban object, both seat and backpack: the STAG, designed to promote the activities and meetings of users who live and work in these in-betweens. In their study they focus their attention on five areas: the space puzzle for the intricate spaces; the flows game

10
The Swedish mathematician Niels Fabian Helge von Koch (1870–1924) is best known for his discovery of what became known as the von Koch snowflake curve. This continuous curve played an important role in the study of fractal geometry.

11
Warren Buffett in an interview with CNN 25 May 2005: "There's class warfare, all right, but it's my class, the rich class, that's making war, and we're winning."

12
Geraldine Borio and Caroline Wüthrich, *Hong Kong In Between*, Zürich: Park Books, 2015 (in Chinese and English).

that animates them; the need for a generous approach to compensate for the nominal narrowness of spaces; the superposition of functions as use maximization strategy; and frugality in the use of materials. This redistribution of cards bets on the emergence of new forms of life and interaction, and proposes to act on these mechanisms only by means of "homeopathic" architecture, in the form of a folding backpack.

This study, which focuses on the modest working populations of the wealthy Asian city-state finds a pertinent extension in a forthcoming work[13] studying the place of the homeless in the city. It is a case study dedicated to another port city, Marseille, and examines from an anthropological point of view how those affected interact within the management of time and space. The emphasis is on the importance of the "comfort" of the homeless in the city, symptomatic of the overall quality of life. These are thought as decisive indicators of its liveability, if not its toxicity; they are understood as the "canaries in the coal mines". The author analyses the deterioration of public space due to the measures taken against the homeless staying in cities. These measures range from the removal of shelters, hidden corners, benches and ledges, and the deliberate planning of inhospitable surfaces that do not afford any appropriation. The thus hardened city will no longer host homeless people and in the same move cease to afford impromptu and free social exchange.

At the same time shopping malls rapidly multiply and with them theme parks and gated communities, all properly standardized, heavily taxed and placed under high surveillance. Indeed, no one stays there without title, debit- or credit card, and everyone goes there with the consent of someone who will be entertained and stripped at the same time.

Contemporary urban planning paid massive blows to a range of delicate spatial features that were conducive to staying in town. The car has helped discriminate and somehow dematerialize space; one moves from a business area to a residential area. The urban expressway bypasses a working-class district on the grounds of convenience and speed; it excludes and thus dissociates entire urban areas, opening the way for inequality of services, jobs and access to prosperity. Planning regulations are like highways: they owe their existence to technical reason and rational neutrality. But, by forcing developers to install basement parking in buildings for example, they transform streets into smooth, hostile corridors pierced by high gates through which one can access residential complexes or offices and the access ramps to the latter's parking spaces. In this context it is not surprising that SUVs are increasingly popular. Their martial air articulates the mental condition in which their drivers and passengers experience the urban environment; for them it is a threatening place in which the strongest wins. Sometimes a particularly brutal manifestation

12
Geraldine Borio and Caroline Wüthrich, *Hong Kong In Between*, Zürich: Park Books, 2015 (in Chinese and English).

13
Chantal Deckmyn, *La Place des SDF dans la ville*, as part of "Lire la ville 2", funded by the Abbé Pierre Foundation and PSA Peugeot-Citroën Foundation – habitat alternatif social; see also an interview with Chantal Deckmyn in *Libération*, 18 January 2016.

of a widespread phenomenon reveals the hidden meaning. In Cartagena de Indias I thoughtfully watched an ordinary yet unique urban scene: on the steps of the cathedral, in flagrant breach of the ban on driving, a "demilitarized" Hummer suddenly emerged. Three private guards inspect the surroundings and the sanctuary, presumably to ensure that God had left the premises before allowing an elegant elderly lady to pass, whose apparent goal was devotion and posting herself menacingly in the "place". This both religious and paramilitary ostentation revealed a terrifying use of the city where members of the ruling class move at high speed from one safe space to another, aware of being a target in an environment that is made uniformly hostile.

Is this what is taught in schools?

"Planning" by university-educated professional planners, taught them so many "good practices", is imposed everywhere. Even when we admit that some schools offer debatable education, there is this persistent impression of a huge gap between the provided education that is often excellent,[14] differentiated or even sophisticated from a theoretical perspective, and the actions of those who enjoyed it from the moment they hold office or have jobs. This question is repeated in its "professional" counterpart stating that education does not correspond to the current practice of the profession and does not sustain a demand for more "realism" and "pragmatism" in courses preparing for architecture and urban planning. What remains is to try to identify the "black hole" in which knowledge and education disappear once their graduated owners get a job or take office. An empirical observation should consider the widest possible range of causes; some have long been known and mainly stick to the expression "the conditions for optimizing land revenues" or trivially: how to make the most money per square metre. This is however not the place to develop this aspect and I would like to focus my attention on a specific factor, indigenous to the practice of the architect, known as the concept of "project" and the extreme focusing on the decontextualized architectural object. The origin could be the Italian Renaissance in which the pictorial realm became objective and based on mathematics, and consequently amalgamated with architectural space. So much so that the architect's clients themselves have come to focus attention on the image of the thing and on the viewpoint. It was an entry in the Blue Guide[15] to the City of Pienza that incidentally delivered me the key. According to this source, Pius II Piccolomini, who built the city, his palace and his cathedral, would have visited the latter at the time of its completion. Having found the cathedral designed by Rossellino perfect in everything and bearing in mind that he himself, the customer, was the sovereign pontiff, he issued a decree threatening to excommunicate anyone who would add or remove anything.

14
For a concise overview of this rich culture taught in schools, the reader can benefit from: *Les Faiseurs de Villes*, texts collected by Thierry Paquot, Gollion: Infolio, 2010.

15
Built on the site of the old Pieve di Santa Maria, the cathedral was oriented differently to fit harmoniously into the plan for the rehabilitation of the historic centre of Pienza, as commissioned by Pope Pius II Piccolomini, born in the village (at that time it was called Corsignano; it was later renamed Pienza in his honour), to make it the architectural example of a Renaissance-style town. Between 1459 and 1462 he entrusted the construction to the architect Bernardo Rossellino.

In doing so, he blessed both the authority of the tandem customer—architect and the fixed nature of the work done. Considered from their "point of view", the manifestation of this extraordinary concentration of power gave it a mythical status. European neoclassical architecture perpetuated this attitude in the eighteenth and nineteenth centuries, blessing and freezing the architectural oeuvre as a finished and intangible thing. From the nineteenth century, theorists of the conservation of monuments have been working to confirm this character and contributed to freezing it in time, making these works a kind of "derivative" object, delivered to a cult.[16] Paradoxically but no less emphatic considering its fundamental aim of reforming housing and the city, modern architecture by its massive use of photography accentuates this phenomenon. Retouchers of architecture photographs[17] had a busy job creating distance to modern architecture's achievements, deleting signs of daily life, birds and even clouds, all not "modern'" enough in their eyes, to make the architecture of object and image acceptable. Curiously, the image would overcome the reformist intent and substance, on the initiative of people like the American Philip Johnson, who reduced the Modern Movement to a "style"[18] in order to have it better focus on its own goals. All these elements, whether they are trivially mundane and follow the slope of the prevailing conditions or are more ideologically elaborate, emphasize the pre-eminence of the project and the designer, and partly explain the conformism and the followership of architects and urban planners in their practices. Very rare are those who deviate from the mainstream, who prefer a delicate and sensible approach, focused on the creation of an urban environment capable of generating life, not just sales. The exception I mentioned above regarding Christopher Alexander however, has theoretical foundations that are even taught in schools. It also has its recognized practitioners: the recent revaluation, on the initiative of Patrick Bouchain, of the work of Simone and Lucien Kroll shows the existence of a true lineage.[19]

The practice of CS Studio Architects as I observed it in the field impressed me enough in terms of attention to the intermediate spaces, to justify these general detours. Their projects consistently show this basic idea and translate it into utterly simple questions: where do the users come from? What makes their day? How long have they been walking in the sun or in the pouring rain? Have they been drinking? What are their physiological, symbolic and social needs at the moment they approach the building that I design for their use: a school, a clinic, a market? What spaces are most capable of meeting their needs?

The system of townships, namely urban areas built during apartheid on the outskirts of South African cities since the late nineteenth century, was a town-planning instrument of policing and racial segregation. It represents

16
Georg Germann, *Aux origines du patrimoine bâti*, Gollion: Infolio, 2009.

17
Antoine Baudin, *Photographie et architecture. La Collection Alberto Sartoris*, Lausanne: PPUR, 2003.

18
Anatole Kopp, *Quand le moderne n'était pas un style mais une cause*, Paris: ENSBA, 1988.

19
Simone and Lucien Kroll, *Une architecture habitée*, ed. Patrick Bouchain, Arles: Actes Sud, 2013.

20
Bruno Jacomy, *Une Histoire des Techniques*, Paris: Seuil, 1990. In particular, Chapter III of Part IV: "Un homme, Francesco di Giorgio Martini."

the most brutal, most primitive urban forms and is directly related to the military origins of the discipline.[20] Since 1994 conditions have changed; the legal framework has changed. The urbanism of segregation was succeeded by bureaucratic and technocratic planning, but the cohesion and discipline that came with the organizations fighting the regime of racial segregation gave way to fragmentation and individualism. In a context of widespread precariousness and the growth of violence, corruption and gangs, CS Studio Architects saw itself confronted with not only the orthogonal aridity of planning but the absolute nonexistence of infrastructure, including mass public transport, as rampant insecurity. This context tested the designers harshly and made them prone to discouragement. Analysis and interpretation of traditional vernacular modes of arrangement of space are a very safe way to continue to organize thinking and allows the development of solutions through increased interaction with users. This principle continues to characterize their projects.

CONSTRUCTION, MATERIALS, RECOVERY: *SOLA DOSIS FACIT VENENUM*

////////

This mantra is recited time and again by the manufacturers of the chemical synthetic molecules used in modern intensive agriculture, plastics and building material in particular. Its formulation is attributed to a certain Philippus Theophrastus Aureolus Bombastus von Hohenheim, the Swiss astrologer and alchemist-physician better known as Paracelsus. If the test of time were sufficient to found a scientific fact, we would know it by now and everything would be simple. It turns out however that his proposition, which until very recently served as paradigm in the development of toxicology, although true in some particular cases, is wrong in principle. The problem is that the effects of some synthetic chemical molecules on living organisms evade toxicological analysis and are only visible for endocrinologists who are aware that chemicals are likely to act like hormones. "About certain chemical products and natural hormones, we know that low doses can stimulate their effects, while large doses inhibit. As for hormones, the dose never makes them poisonous and the effects don't worsen systematically since in endocrinology linear dose-response curves do not exist."[1]

This finding has considerable consequences since it entirely disqualifies the fanciful notion of "acceptable daily intake" (ADI), which is the basis of authoritative procedures for market introduction of synthetic chemical molecules. ADI participates in a perverse process of reverse onus, under which manufacturers are exempt from the undeniable demonstration of the safety of their products, but at the proven expense of the health of users on whose shoulders the burden of demonstrating their harmfulness and health consequences eventually falls. For a very long time, the building materials industry has relied on collected, harvested or extracted natural resources. However, "natural" does not mean "safe", as became clear from the drama of products containing asbestos fibres, banned in Switzerland since 1989. To a large extent, the emphasis given to these public health tragedies comes from a recurrent interference of boasting about the advancement of knowledge and promoting the idea that the progress of science nowadays can prevent such disasters. This propaganda is belied by the facts. On the one hand, the number of chemical molecules that go into the composition of building materials has soared in the last thirty years and, although many of them were withdrawn after their toxic nature was demonstrated (formaldehyde, PCBs, lindane, etc.), numerous volatile organic compounds (VOCs) (benzene, toluene, xylene, phenol, formaldehyde, ketones, acetones, etc.) are still being used in the production of paints, varnishes, carpets, coatings, adhesives, and especially insulating materials. The latter category is soaring in terms of volume and turnover since standards and quality labels now govern, under the virtuous cover of energy saving, the field of prescribed investment in the construction industry.

1 Marie-Monique Robin, *Notre poison quotidien : la responsabilité de l'industrie chimique dans l'épidémie des maladies chroniques*, Paris: Arte édition-La Découverte, 2013, interview by the author with Fred vom Saal, a biologist at Columbia College, Missouri, 387.

Not only exposure to these pollutants is regulated with the inadequate paradigmatic concept of the "acceptable daily intake", but it turns out that on the wind of deregulating neoliberalism the ensemble of regulatory bodies, state certification bureaus and university laboratories has come under tremendous pressure from the chemical industry. It is no exaggeration to say that researchers and truly independent authorities have become a minority and the butt of a wide range of manoeuvres to ostracize and disqualify them. The detailed mechanisms described by Marie-Dominique Robin let shivers run down one's spine as so much imposes the banal nature of "evil" itself as well as the deeply institutionalized nature of the conditions in which it unfolds. While the problem is acute in highly developed countries, equipped with structured public institutions and insensitive to corruption, it takes monstrous proportions in those where there is absolute *laissez-faire* and where democracy is absent.

Yielding to attractive professional "information", engineers and architects prescribe "contemporary" materials without much regard to their chemical composition, and thus their impact on construction workers and users, not to mention the life cycle of materials or the grey energy that is encapsulated in it. The construction industry is developing with spectacular impetuosity everywhere, draining huge amounts of capital; it only cares about ethics and environmental impact if the democratic debate forces it to do so.

CS Studio Architects has developed an acute awareness of these mechanisms and experimented in a pragmatic, intuitive and opinionated way with many approaches in order to escape from it, anticipating for almost thirty years on what research and publications nowadays embrace fairly accurately.[2] Architects finely articulate countless detailed practices, all of which contribute to the "sustainability" of their buildings. They act on qualification of the workforce (local jobs, techniques that support learning processes), on the origin and nature of materials (local resources, local orders, money circulation within communities) and are part of the site by taking advantage of their bioclimatic characteristics and allowing the reuse of structures, constructions, or elements already in place.

The battle of the dressers

In architecture, as in all manifestations of life on earth, basically everything is being reused.[3]

Even after globalization has deployed most of its effects, a territory is still characterized as the unity of place in which the activities of individuals of our species take place. It is where they drink, feed, breed and build their homes. In a famous article, the late André Corboz[4] called the territory a "palimpsest" bearing the traces of its successive occupations. We can basically see it as the first and most fundamental of forms of re-use, one containing them all, the one that

2
See especially the overview provided by *VERSUS: Heritage for Tomorrow. Vernacular Knowledge for Sustainable Architecture*, *op. cit.*

3
I am confining myself to only the term "reuse". Whereas the distinction according to which "reuse" can be understood as the case in which the same use is made of the re-used object, the term "recycling" is a misnomer since it is in insurmountable contradiction with the second law of thermodynamics.

4
André Corboz, *Le Territoire comme palimpseste et autres essais*, Paris: L'Imprimeur, 2001.

defines them. In the age of the Anthropocene[5] and of Caterpillar machines, we observe that the oldest layers of the palimpsest tend to disappear because of the violence of the applied means; we are witnessing the realization of the mythical *tabula rasa*. The territorial dimension of the act of building was the natural choice in prehistoric times, in a constrained symbiosis with the environment. Our ancestors practised "bioclimatic" architecture by default. The founding narratives of the history of architecture evoke "Adam's house in paradise"[6] and "the story of a house".[7] Both are chronicles of a building act that basically consisted of taking advantage of available resources, often without transforming them, and of optimizing the characteristics of the buildings and thus meeting the principles that Vitruvius pointed out: *firmitas* (strength) *utilitas* (utility) and *venustas* (beauty). In the context of scarcity that characterizes Antiquity and the Middle Ages, reuse of building materials was not only widespread practice, but somehow a matter of course that became part of common sense just as easy since the prerogatives of ownership, in the absence of a land register and a rigorously precise legal framework, were less systematically practised than today. The ruin of a palace, once the dynasty that built it was absent, ousted or defeated, tended to return to the rank of "common good" and thus of available resource. We can distinguish several categories of reuse practices: the simplest case is the collection of elements from a building in ruins, followed by their integration into a new building, often for a functional and structural use similar to the original design. This way of renewing form and function extends the useful life of the initial effort. CS Studio Architects has applied this strategy in many cases, including recovering steel structures of collective residential buildings under apartheid destined for mass housing of workers. In doing so, CS Studio Architects not only recovers a constructive element, but also induced a memorial evocation; the roof that once covered suffering now hosts a useful function for the community. The symbolic value becomes a plus, as stressed afterwards by critics. The most widespread practice of reuse is to treat the ancient ruins as a quarry or a mine. The reused material is either simply retracted from view, or outright treated as raw material that then participates in a more or less complex transformation process consuming more or less energy. Deplored are the marbles of Pergamum and Rome that fed the mouths of lime kilns for centuries. The rubble of late twentieth century South Africa may not evoke the same romantic regrets, but the method is similar.

Nothing new under the sun

CS Studio Architects has done original work in its pragmatic search for solutions that are reasonable and consistent with its objectives. What they did was pure pioneering, outside any organized structure, like the local

5
Claude Lorius and Laurent Carpentier, *Voyage dans l'Anthropocène, cette nouvelle ère dont nous sommes les héros*, Arles: Actes Sud, 2010. The term "Anthropocene" is controversial, although it reflects a tangible reality; Vandana Shiva sees it as an arrogant assertion of the empire of our species on the world.

6
Joseph Rykwert, *On Adam's House in Paradise the Idea of the Primitive Hut in Architectural History*, New York: Museum of Modern Art, 1972.

7
Eugène-Emmanuel Viollet-le-Duc, *Histoire d'une maison*, Paris: Hetzel, 1873.

CAI IP

reuse networks found for example in Belgium and throughout Europe. Contemporary developments that consider waste as a mineral resource [8] were not common practice yet. Every methodical and far-sighted practice of recycling, on whatever scale implemented, inevitably ends up running into three fundamental problems:

- The law of entropy, which states that nothing can be recycled, i.e. that everything degrades;
- The need to mobilize huge amounts of energy for these mining and refining processes;
- The idea that separating into original materials, as virtuous and attractive as it is may sound, is ultimately an illusion. Philippe Bihouix [9] gives a telling example. According to him, "95% of the titanium extracted worldwide is used as a universal white pigment. It is found everywhere, in plastics, toothpaste, sunscreen, paint... and impossible to retrieve. The same goes for a part of the world's chromium, cobalt, zinc and antimony. "Urban mining techniques are especially important in a context that leaves hyper-urbanization not only to be considered by most experts as a "natural phenomenon", but above all to be promoted to the rank of unique universal model of territorial development. In all cases, the city is the essential territorial unit of reuse. The city determines the deep, intrinsic nature of the mineral resources it concentrates and rejects; their quality of "ore" is directly related to its level of development, prosperity, and organization. Very few people are aware of the extent to which this process corresponds primarily to the vertical structure of power required by contemporary financial capitalism and land grabbing by institutional investors, large companies or very wealthy individuals. In essence, the domain of reuse is neither innocent nor particularly peaceful and can lead to severe confrontations. The phrase "to fight like rag-and-bone men" refers to documented episodes [10] in the collection of raw materials for the paper industry before 1830. Such collection was a potential source of violent conflict fed by information about the price the rag-and-bone men were likely to ask for their waste material.

Within the contemporary urban territory, the conditions are nowadays such that highly conflicting systems gather around the collection and recovery of reusable materials. We see in fact on one side the advocates of recovering a vernacular domain, [11] that is to say often the militants of associative and solidarity groups interested in self-production and self-consumption of resources for the art of building. On the other side we see industry groups that have already put the profit potential held by the mountain of rejected waste into operation. CS Studio Architects has experienced these mechanisms painfully and in detail. Not only was the

8
See the numerous occurrences of urban mining available on the Internet, particularly the symposium: http://urban-mining.it/.

9
Philippe Bihouix, *L'Âge des low tech. Vers une civilisation techniquement soutenable*, Paris: Seuil, 2014. In *Libération*, 5–6 July 2014, "Idées grand format", 28–29.

10
See Erik Orsenna, *Sur la route du papier. Petit précis de mondialisation III*, Paris: Stock, 2012.

11
Ivan Illich, *Gender*, London: Boyars, 1983.

methodical demolition of the Ulwazi school, right next to the Guga S'Thebe community centre, commissioned by a contractor involved in the reinforced concrete market with its financial flows that help maintain corruption, but the sponsor would also have pushed the evil by encouraging the big guys who were hired for this operation, to "feast on the beast" by selling the materials from the demolition!

Even waste is only available in finite quantities

This explanation would benefit from further elaboration and clarification but there is no room for that here. It is implicitly based on the idea that the resources of planet earth, especially the vital resources like a breathable atmosphere, drinking water and arable land, are only available in finite quantities. Consequently, not only our existence as a species is closely dependent on them; also our actions and our way of allowing or otherwise preventing the overuse of these resources need to be analysed and understood. Moreover, their equitable distribution requires governance. CS Studio Architects works according paradigms that fully integrate this kind of concerns. It is fascinating to identify the structuring elements in the ensemble of their built work.

Finally, the only question that matters is whether humanity will prove capable of allocating the resources of a finite world, thus rationing them, or whether it will hand itself over to the savage rationing by the markets. Anthropology primarily, but other disciplines as well, has sought to understand and explain the regulatory systems that human societies use to manage the allocation of available resources and wealth; more or less unequal conditions, as well as religious or ideological paradigms adopted by different societies determine their ability to overcome the challenges they face: in particular those related to environmental degradation and climate change. The author of *Collapse*[12] attempts to identify the conditions that make a society overcome the challenge of managing its resources or, conversely, precipitate its demise. According to him, these conditions specifically determine success or failure, collapse or survival; they measure the level of resilience a society manages to put out.

We believe that faced with the finite availability of vital resources, the passengers of Spaceship Earth[13] will seal their fate and survival with the way they treat the allocation of these resources. In the modern era, the long history of humankind has taken a radical turn with unforeseeable consequences. Population growth and entry into modernity, facilitated by scientific thinking and rational organization of knowledge, have forced societies to fundamentally change their modes of allocating the right to exploit natural resources. The chosen direction is fraught with threats. The development of law reflects precisely the taken direction. It took off with the transition from the regime of natural law to that of positive law. In France this process

12
Jared Diamond, *Collapse: How Societies Choose to Fail or Succeed*, New York: Viking, 2005.

13
Richard Buckminster Fuller, *Operating Manual for Spaceship Earth*, ed. Jaime Snyder, Baden: Lars Müller Publishers, 2008.

started in the wake of the Revolution and stabilized in the first two decades of the nineteenth century. "Nature [has become] a battlefield":[14] courts began to admit that the destruction of a free natural resource, that is to say a common good, could be the subject of financial compensation, provided that the victims are able to provide proof of the harm they have suffered. In the modern era, this mechanism actually turns nature into a commodity; it is the origin of today's "pollution rights". This development obviously does not stand alone; as earth gradually enters the Anthropocene,[15] the competition model that governs the allocation of resources becomes fiercer and more violent. It tends to extend to all types of resources. Humanity not only imposes its grip and control of resources on other species[16] whereas in fairness it should ration access to resources, on the contrary it delivers them to the speculative and murderous madness of the markets. Thanks to the economic and trade mechanisms and rules imposed by neoliberalism, resources are now subject to speculation, which is ultimately no more than rationing dominated by price. Thus, with this "triumph of greed",[17] societies disintegrate and close the bill with "the price of inequality".[18] Today, not only are we still not moving towards a fair solution negotiated between peoples or nations, but neoliberalism, which since the 1970s has gradually taken over the main levers of power, leads us to the exact opposite and thus tends to precipitate the disaster.

For the problem addressed here, this aspect is of fundamental importance because it allows us to understand which forces play a role in the enormous market being formed, with waste understood as an "ore". Under the title *Du rare à l'infini. Panorama mondial des déchets*,[19] a professor at Université Paris-Dauphine has published a study on the evolution of "waste markets" in 135 countries. The preface informs us that its "scientific research" was funded by an industrial environmental group that controls the water supply of many local communities. For their part, governments play a key role in this. They are in charge of public hygiene and sanitation, including the collection and sorting of all kinds of waste, as well as their newly introduced "recoverability". They also hold, in principle, the monopoly of coercive force. Public policies are usually implemented under the guise of technical and managerial rigour. Here and there, criticism is heard on the tendency to blame the users rather than to address the source of the waste (manufacturers and retail). Some target the deferral of expenses that tends to make the last link of the chain pay, as in the good old technique of musical chairs. However, few and far between are the observers who identified the real issue in this case, namely how to pinpoint the moment when the waste collected by local authorities at the expense of the taxpayer, becomes an "urban ore" to be sold on a controlled market, i.e. manipulated by private groups dominating the sector. The analysis cited

14
Jean-Baptiste Fressoz, *L'Apocalypse joyeuse. Une histoire du risque technologique*, Paris : Seuil, 2012. See also: Razmig Keucheyan, *La nature est un champ de bataille. Essai d'écologie politique*, Paris: Zones, 2014.

15
See note 5.

16
Keith Thomas, *Man and the Natural World: Changing Attitudes in England 1500–1800*, Harmondsworth: Penguin Books, 1984.

17
Joseph E. Stiglitz, *Freefall: America, Free Markets, and the Sinking of the World Economy*. New York: W. W. Norton & Co, 2010.

18
Joseph E. Stiglitz, *The Price of Inequality: How Today's Divided Society Endangers Our Future*, New York: W. W. Norton & Co, 2012.

19
Philippe Chalmin and Catherine Gaillochet, *Du rare à l'infini. Panorama mondial des déchets 2009*, Paris: Economica, 2009.

above evokes in vivid detail, and with obvious eagerness, that the emerging waste markets are unstable and fluctuating. It is a small step from there to speculating on price movements and selling off the "urban ore". There is no doubt that this will happen as soon as the opportunity arises. It will be the ultimate development in this process since wherever capitalism has identified significant sources of profit, it worked on liquidating the "common" and creating monopolies.

This economic logic is doubly perverse. First, it massively mortgages the development of reuse networks and reduces their scope, looming as a competitor naturally inclined to limit or even prohibit the practice. Under the guise of technical and health and safety standards, small skimmers are denied access to demolition sites. Secondly, it tends to legitimize and "think positive of" waste production itself. To the extent that it has become "ore" and that no one cares about the by-products or the excessive amount of energy required by the transformation process, the new waste economy is likely to boost their availability, to trivialize their existence, which on a global scale frontally contravenes the necessary frugality our species should now show.

In this general context, the empirical reuse practices such as CS Studio Architects is used to implement, face contingent as well as conceptual obstacles. We must struggle and go ahead, both in the reality of the first order as in the formulation of utopia. This requires overcoming the "Looking for Eric syndrome" that struck the viewers of Ken Loach's film,[20] torn between their perception of reality and their desire to dream. For this reason, we must take time to expose the observed facts to the weapons of criticism.

20 Ken Loach (dir.), *Looking for Eric*, 2009.

THE WONDERFUL RESOURCES OF ARCHITECTURE, THE FAITH IN THE BRAZILIAN FUTURE OF THE WORLD

/////////

"Culture is the product of a people's history. But it also reflects that history, and embodies a whole set of values by which people view themselves and their place in space and time."[1] This quotation has played an important role in the conceptual development of the work of CS Studio Architects.[2] Pointing to the fact that sustainable development is primarily addressed "in a technological approach that implements sophisticated solutions, expensive and difficult to maintain", CS Studio Architects explains it has focused its architectural practice in South Africa on the observation of traditional spatial practices, on how to operate on the terrain of different cultures. This anthropological approach to traditional built space has revealed the resources of highly complex and interesting features. It gave room to an architecture clearly in tune with deconstructivism in the 1990s, but did so by equipping it with a legitimacy drawn from the roots of local cultures, implemented with Vitruvian rigor.

Also on the agency's website it says: "rural vernacular architecture provides solutions which are extremely interesting and relevant which are closely related to urban informal settlements. ... A traditional village is made up of a number of structures which are spaced apart, with most of the social interactive spaces being outside. The structures are also placed with the doors facing east to bring in the morning sunlight. Roofs hang over the mud walls to protect them from rain while also shading them. It is a perfect system of natural materials, natural use of light and it is thermally appropriate. The way in which the buildings are ordered and placed in the landscape also provides valuable information regarding social and cultural structures. In most traditional examples the use of decoration is important. ... In the urban context it is the same spatial use of juxtaposing smaller units in such a way to create useful in-between spaces. When studying an aerial photograph one sees the intermediate social spaces. CS Studio Architects have found the above aspects useful when planning any architectural solution from a town planning exercise, for example the housing village at Caledon Helderstroom Prison, to the school at Wesbank, Guga S'thebe Cultural Village and Commercial Centre Follainville – Dennemont, France."

These statements are fundamental; they are the substance of a practice that has broken away from both the ideology of architectural form and the principles of urban planning based on regulatory autism. Taking benefit from these interstitial spaces intensifies their use, increases social interaction, and yields significant savings. But this spatial economy by itself is not enough; it works only because its irrational character opens the fractal dimension needed for the expression of diversity. The world of forms and colours implemented by CS Studio Architects feeds on disrupted perspectives and space fragmentation; gold, bright reds and emerald greens are unthinkable on solids and orthogonal shapes; they cannot co-exist or deploy their

1
Wa Thiong'o Ngugi, *Moving the Centre: The Struggle for Cultural Freedoms*, Portsmouth, NH: Heinemann, 1993. Ngugi is a Kenyan writer born in 1938, professor and director of the International Center for Writing and Translation, University of California, Irvine. He is particularly known for *Decolonising the Mind* (1986).

2
"Our Philosophy", CS Studio Architects, http://csstudio.co.za/Philosophy.html.

effects with them. Thanks to the forms and colours that articulate them, the spaces created by CS Studio Architects churn out habitats where life finds freedom. En passant, the description of this phenomenon says something about the obligatory hygienic in which modernism falls back on the sinister and aptly named Salubra gamut, perfectly in tune with spatial Corbusian eugenics.

In the same movement of reference to vernacular architecture from which it draws its lessons, CS Studio Architects is inspired by circular shapes that can "challenge the traditional square-based arrangements and [to] facilitate other juxtapositions of elements, as in Africa many traditional cultures inhabited houses with circular plans. These traditions in the appropriation of space are obviously linked to belief systems. These arrangements structured in layers or successive circles are richer than the traditional European framework based on three-dimensional representation. They reflect the cultural diversity. This is an aspect of particular importance at a time when migration has become the norm."[3] CS Studio Architects believes that "respect and integration of cultural diversity is the key to producing a quality urban environment".

From 60 degrees north to 34 degrees south

CS Studio Architects' architecture feeds on the coincidence and willpower of two architects whose paths converged in the course of the 1980s in a large Cape Town architecture firm. As a teenager, Carin Smuts following a vital élan, broke with the ideology of apartheid and took advantage of the opening to the world given to her by her aunt, the eminent and atypical veterinary medicine professor at the University of Pretoria, Malie Smuts.[4] Urs Schmid pulled into the world and put aside the closely codified setting of a small town in German-speaking Switzerland, where the vocational track of learning, as strong as it was, limited his development. With an unerring instinct, he went off to Scandinavia where the "second modern" in architecture was being written with tenderness and fantasy. While the world could go along two axes, he chose the vertical and went to South Africa.

From the very beginning, CS Studio Architects' social commitment is based on a simple and obvious idea: racial discrimination is absolutely unacceptable. It must be fought in all its manifestations and this commitment must be translated into action. As for them, their action is architecture, in its diversity and indivisible unity, in the richness of its issues. At all times they considered the field of their work indistinguishable from that of social activism. CS Studio Architects was a white pioneer in the fight against the politics of apartheid, the architects acted as genuine fellow activists against apartheid, even in the underground movement and facing tragic events before 1990. It is characteristic of horizons to think they are insurmountable,

3
Ibid.

4
Malie M. S. Smuts (1938), author of a pioneering reference book: *Anatomy of the Dromedary*, Oxfordshire: Oxford Science Publishers, 1987.

whereas it is characteristic of visionaries to belie this semblance. Paradoxically, it was after 1994 that things got complicated. The historic adversary had retired to its globalized bastions, the old white elite kept control over financial capital while the power of the state, provinces and municipalities was transferred to those who were once discriminated against. The rainbow nation could adopt the hope of a creolization of its human population, as in 2009 formulated by Chamoiseau and Glissant in *L'Intraitable Beauté du Monde*, and that Coetzee's autobiographical fiction would resume the same year in *Summertime*. However, as in all neo-colonial areas, the emancipation of the oppressed masses of the Republic of South Africa got stuck in the swamp of corruption. The latter spread like wildfire, fuelled by the sudden abundance of capital and the scintillating supply of goods pouring down on people who had been wronged for a long time. The horizontal integration process involving architects, population, historical activists and historical community chiefdoms was if not completely stopped, at least severely hampered. To stay on track with the particular and virtuoso way of making architecture characteristic of CS Studio Architects, became difficult and often discouraging in the context of a world that bureaucratized at high speed in a kind of unbridled public-private partnership.[5] On the one hand, the supply of high-value globalized building materials imposes its constraints and standards, while on the other hand an administration living off past injustices ensures the implementation of "best practices". The trap is almost perfect, even if the story is not finished yet. Within EPFL,[6] which hosted my career as an archivist, historian and architectural critic, a settled observer and recognized virtuoso of equivocation, exclaimed one day, exasperated by my relentless criticism: "His problem is that he does not like architecture!" He simply could not square a constant and rigorous high level of exactingness with a strong faith in Vitruvian morality. In conclusion I mean here that with CS Studio Architects I finally found architecture as it should be, making my heart beat faster. Forged in CS Studio Architects, the immense and persistent talent of Carin Smuts and Urs Schmid is, through defecting and the abandonment of prerogatives, the ability to successfully deploy without any concession, architecture that treats volumes and light by frugal yet virtuoso implementation of the humblest materials.

5
In this regard, the reader could refer to the amazing book by David Graeber, *The Utopia of Rules: On Technology, Stupidity, and the Secret Joys of Bureaucracy*. Brooklyn, NY: Melville House, 2015.

6
Swiss Federal Institute of Technology Lausanne, Switzerland.

PRIMARY SCHOOL FOR 400 CHILDREN AND PUBLIC LIBRARY,
CRADOCK, EASTERN CAPE, 1982-1989, CS STUDIO ARCHITECTS
/////////

All CS Studio Architects' DNA can be found in their first project in Cradock. While that DNA is already fully deployed in this project, in successive projects its rich potential will be gradually revealed.

It all began in 1982 through the initiative of eight black migrant workers, a man and seven women, and a professor of architecture at the University of Cape Town. When they asked the latter for help in providing their community with basic public facilities, essential for its development, the professor suggests the subject to one of his students, Carin Smuts. The community, located in Cradock 250 kilometres north of Port Elizabeth, was engaged in a long story of struggle for emancipation, to which it was about to add a tragic and sensational page. The story in particular brings back the names of the CRADOYA (Cradock Youth Association) and mathematics professor Matthew Goniwe, who was assassinated together with three other activists[1] in 1985, in an ambush set up by the South African police. The "village" of Cradock was severely segregated by the apartheid policy and consisted of a black township separated from an ultra-conservative white rural community by a buffer zone, meant to absolutely prevent contact between ethnic groups.

All administration was in the hands of whites, so even charitable fundraising for a black community project was subject to bureaucratic constraints in the form of collection permits controlled by whites. Access to land was simply forbidden to blacks and the entire process of the project took place not only six hours away from Cape Town, where the architect was finishing her studies, but in clandestine conditions created by the apartheid regime. It pitted a young white woman from a family that ruled the country, with black men and women determined to conquer the means needed for a decent life and fight, with all hazards, the regime that enslaved them.

Under such circumstances, the role of the architect has no relation whatsoever with the terms of an assignment that the teachers of a school of architecture can understand. As for the client, they find themselves even further from the usual standards, insofar that they have no building land, and neither credit nor administrative and technical contacts (land register, surveyor, notary, etc.) to properly manage the project. The "customer", a collective entity in the process of aggregating, also has no representation of its needs and must invent everything from scratch, including the ability to name things, to give substance to the imagination, and to build confidence in its ability to achieve what seems literally impossible.

The architects understand their role as a catalyst of a barely formulated collective ambition, as a vector of knowledge, knowing, know-how and culture, which they apply in a collective process of which they can control neither pace nor timing. Moreover, the process is regularly hampered by the repressive agenda of the white powers. Therefore, the approach cannot be oriented on

1
Known as the "Cradock Four", on 27 June 1985 Matthew Goniwe, Sparrow Mkhonto, Fort Calata and Sicelo Mhlaui were intercepted by police on the way to Port Elizabeth and killed and burned in the vehicle they were travelling in.

the project, but must focus entirely on the process. The educated architect's usual pallet appears of limited use:

- Models and typologies are at best exotic, they induce aberrations and illusions; new forms of spatial arrangement must be invented, which correspond to the culture of its users and stimulate creativity.
- The historical types most often imply authoritarian use or are perceived as such.
- Spaces, scarce and expensive, must be able to host a variety of activities.
- Scale is readily seen as a key element in giving size to the items that need a place.

As for Carin Smuts, by then an architecture student about to finish her studies, the process will be described in a classic anti-academic way, in terms of a manifesto for reform of the school of architecture.

The years 1982–1986 were marked by the confrontation of the actors with a score of incredible obstacles. Fundraising was allowed but limited to a geographical area inhabited by an ultra-conservative white community, so in practice it was impossible. As for the generosity of foreign embassies, like that of the United States in this case, it was limited to the prescription of prefabricated elements. The authorities attributed land in the buffer zone but frustrated its clear definition and demarcation, and when the markers were finally placed, they were immediately vandalized by vehicles belonging to the security forces. Most members of the black community who were engaged in the process became the target of prosecution or direct persecution. Under a regime of rigorous curfew, meetings were highly illegal. Despite these obstacles the architect succeeded in not only setting up a horizontal and democratic process that allowed things as simple as "getting to know" and "taking the time to interact", but also to establish "a common understanding of intentions and the project's content" and to judge its "validity, its importance for the community".

Formulated in a simple and accessible way, the theoretical assumptions of the architect matched or at least were inspired by those of Christopher Alexander: "A building is primarily a physical object, while its success is measured primarily by its use", wrote Carin Smuts in her master's thesis,[2] which consisted of an account of her fieldwork experiences in Cradock. The construction of the first phase with a crèche for 400 children as a target did not really begin until 1986. Then it was completed the same year and immediately followed by the second phase, which would produce a library. The site faced the same obstacles as the crèche and highlighted an interesting aspect, namely how a library project in such conditions becomes the catalyst for a staff-training process and the creation of jobs. These questions were part of the project's debate and as a result, everything went very much as if the end users' own employment had managed to invite itself to the construction site.

2
All the above quotations are from Carin Smuts' master's thesis in architecture, "Process vs. Product, Architectural Work in a Developing Context", University of Cape Town, September 1991.

When visiting these buildings almost twenty-five years later, bearing in mind that everything in the procedure could have been determined by the conditions experienced by the community and adapted to the quite dramatic and exceptional circumstances, it is striking to see how the DNA of CS Studio Architects has not only permeated the process but also enabled the specific alchemy of interactions to succeed. It clearly defines the phenotypes of its architecture: construction, structuring of space, direction of light, volumes, spatial arrangements and colours; everything is present and recognizable. The architecture of CS Studio Architects was born in Cradock and through all its developments and variations, it will surely last throughout the studio's career.

WESBANK, PRIMARY SCHOOL,
KUILS RIVER, WESTERN CAPE, 1989-2002,
CS STUDIO ARCHITECTS /////////

The primary school in this new neighbourhood was designed to accommodate 1,120 children and to provide the local community with a semi-independent service area. It consists of a multipurpose hall, a library, computer services and a community kitchen. The ensemble offers security and protection to its users in an area marked by gangs and high crime rates. Various sports facilities and outdoor spaces included in the compound complete the design.

The idea for the pattern of the plan is that of a medieval village, with the sheltering spaces it offers to its residents in addition to the "houses" they inhabit. Classrooms are grouped in units on a single level for younger pupils and on two levels for older students. They are connected by irregularly shaped walkways, which provide shelter in winter and rainy periods, as well as protection against the heat of summer. The classrooms are arranged along these passages and close the space off from the outside and create the many interstitial small yards and courtyards where both organized and spontaneous activities can take place.

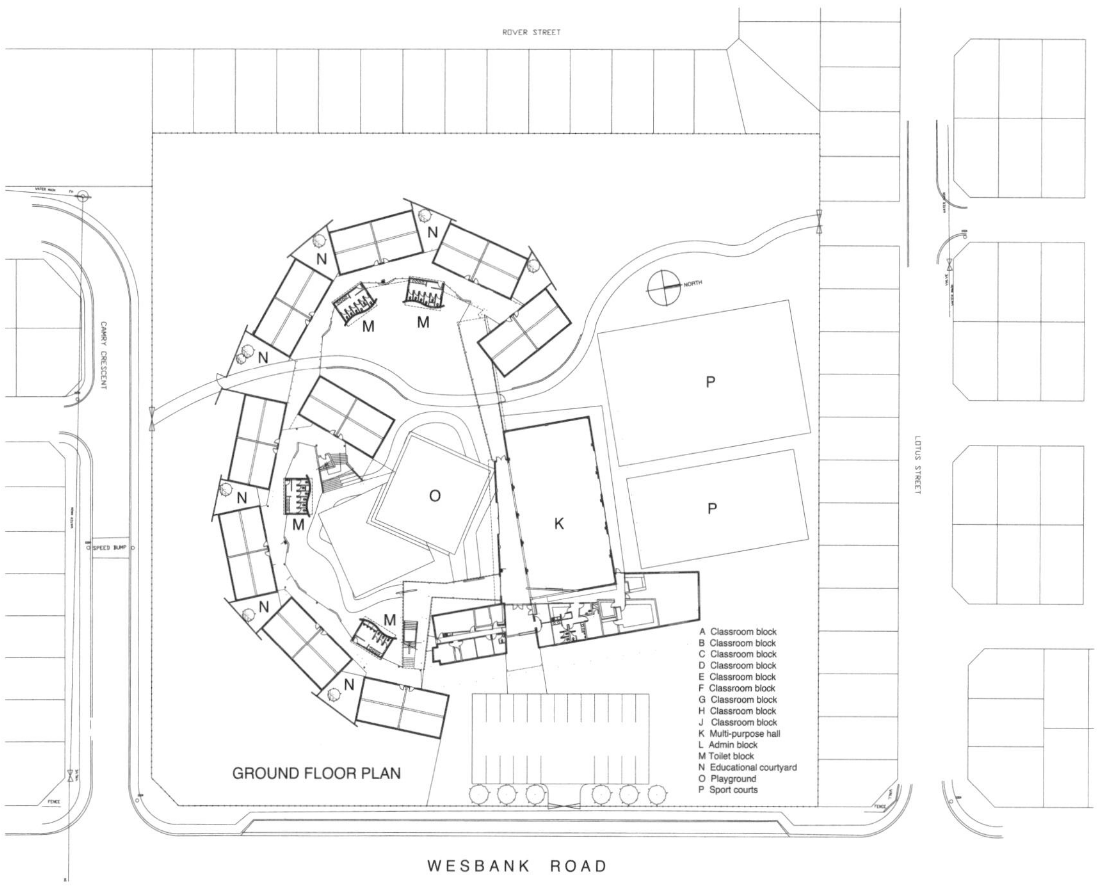

Strolling through this project the many tricks the architects have applied, always using the simplest means, can be seen. The students' toilet block, for example, fully respects the privacy of its users but allows teachers to exercise their monitoring without leaving their classroom.

The brickwork cavity walls put their mass against the rains that beat them horizontally, while the roof structures come from the beams and cladding industry. Surfaces plastered in bright colours mark specific areas and functions. Everywhere light is directed with great precision, providing a sense of homogeneity along the differentiation of space. Entering, leaving, going or getting somewhere, every step is marked by a bright atmosphere, making it a real CS Studio signature.

Fifteen years after its opening, the extremely popular school—some classrooms host two complete courses during the same day—is in immaculate condition. This is undoubtedly due to the respect the poor have for vital equipment. The quality of construction certainly plays a role. Finishing is chosen with rigorous economy; one finds no excessive technique or design.

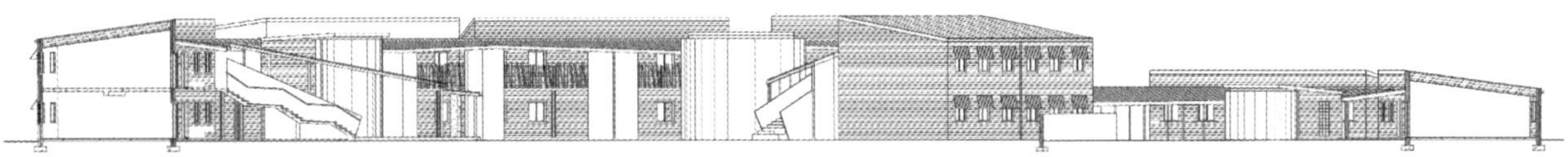

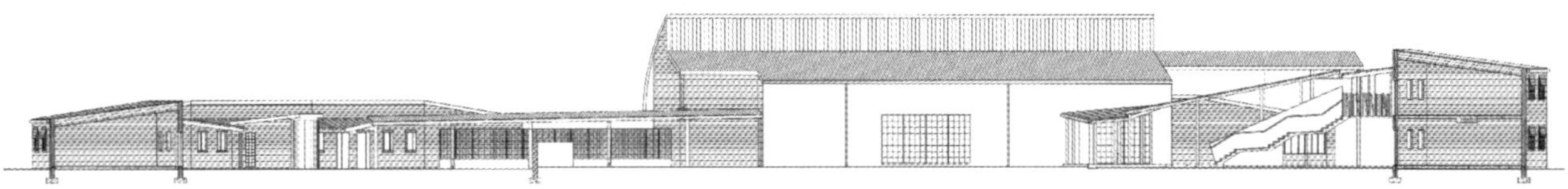

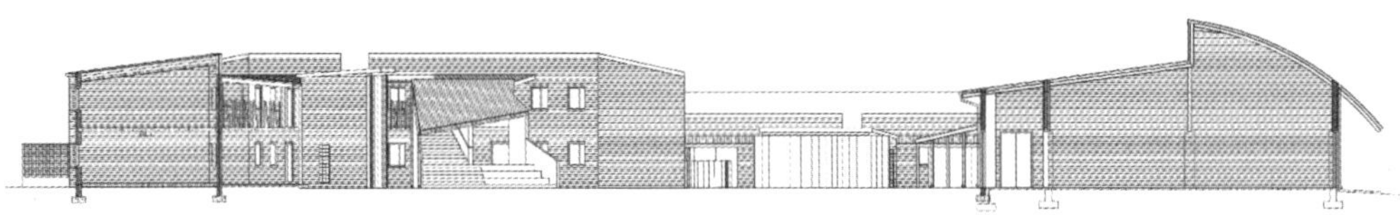

HELSINKI CENTRAL PUBLIC LIBRARY,
FINLAND, A TWO-STAGE COMPETITION,
2012, CS STUDIO ARCHITECTS /////////

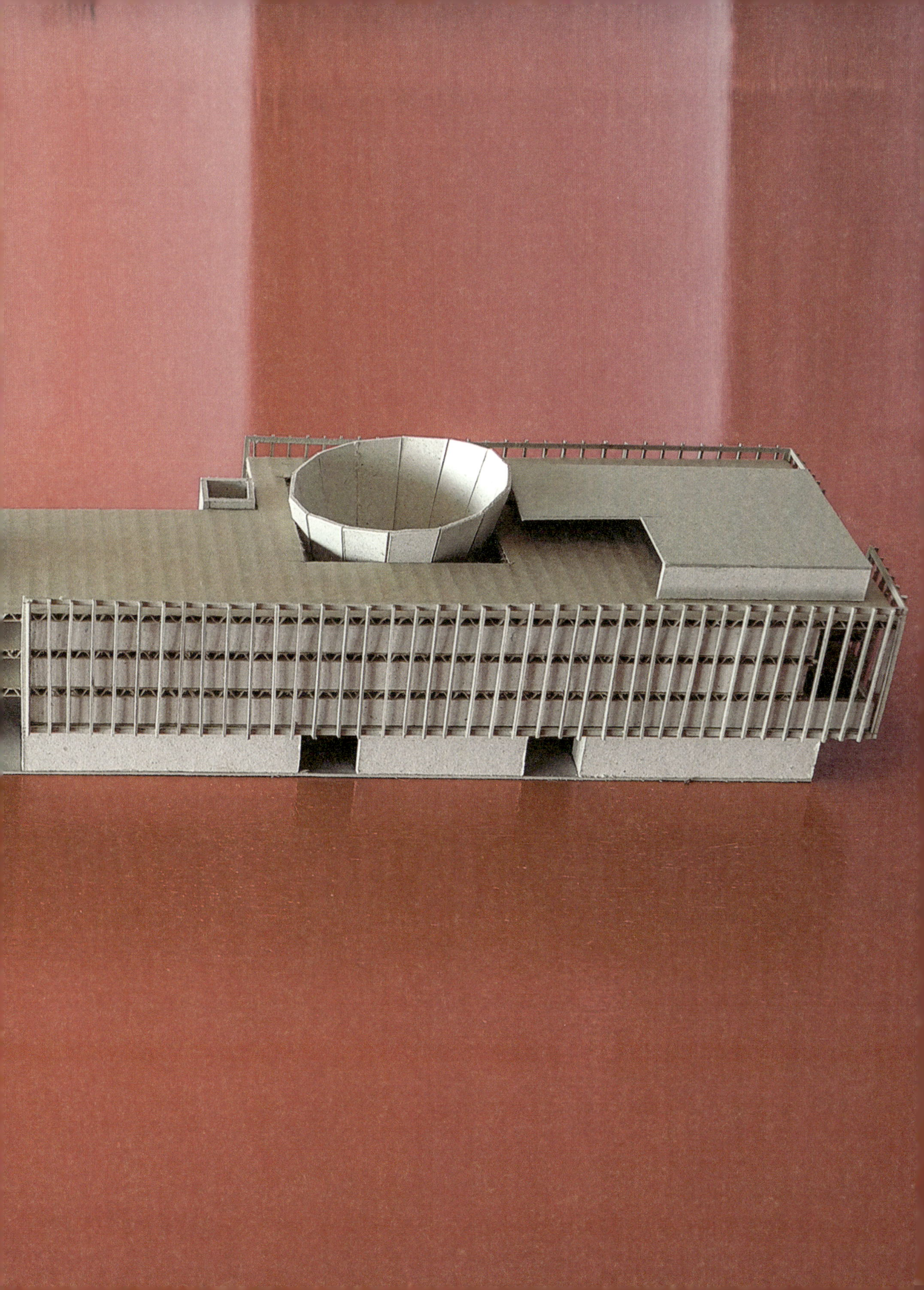

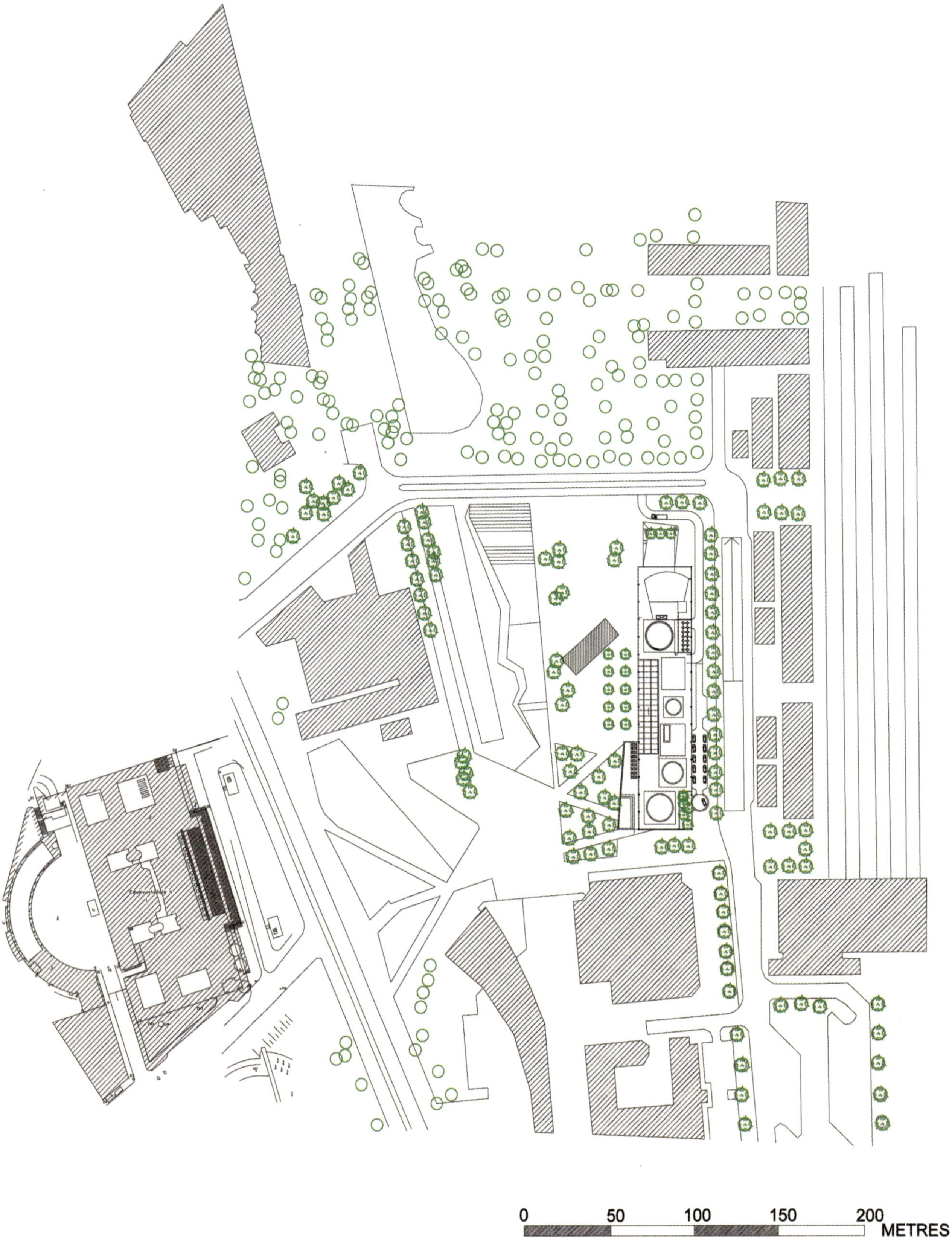
0
50
100
150
200
METRES

During 2012 Helsinki was World Design Capital, and a two-stage architecture competition was one of the outstanding parts of this event. It served both a political and a patriotic purpose, the celebration of Finland's centenary of independence in 2017. The importance of this event can be clearly understood, bearing in mind that Finland's place between its powerful neighbours, Sweden and Russia, has imposed episodes of war that have deeply marked the country's spirit. After independence the Russo-Finnish wars became part of the European collective imagination.

The aim of this two-stage competition was to select a project for a library to be built in the heart of City Block 2014, not far from the railway station known from Jim Jarmusch's movie *Night on Earth* and in the immediate vicinity of the Finnish Parliament, the Helsinki Music Centre, Alvar Aalto's Finlandia Hall, Sanoma House and the Kiasma Museum of Contemporary Art, thus in a highly meaningful context.

FRONT ELEVATION

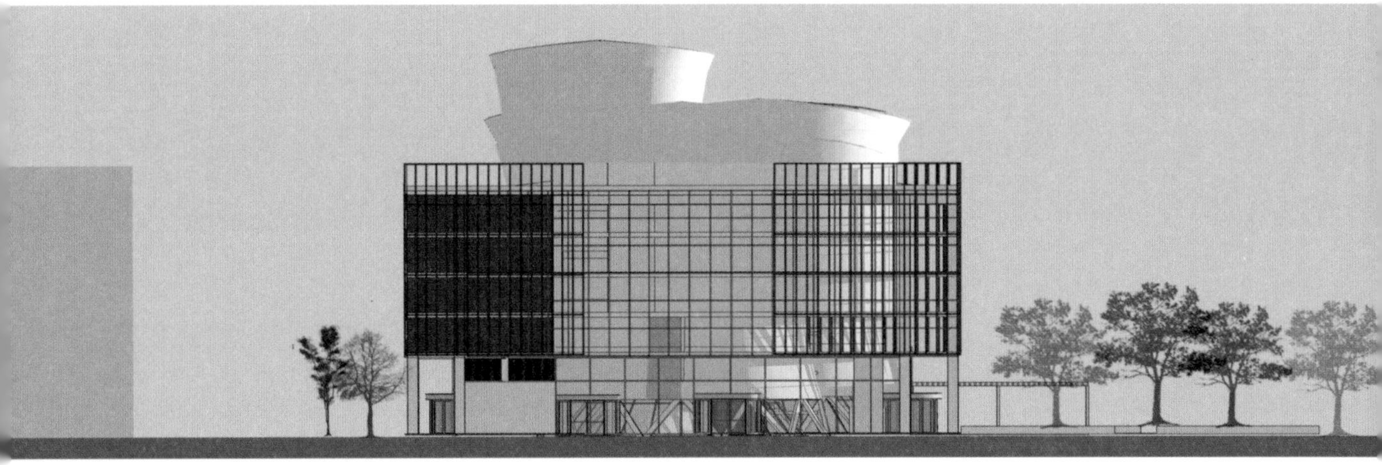

SIDE ELEVATION

BACK ELEVATION

SIDE ELEVATION

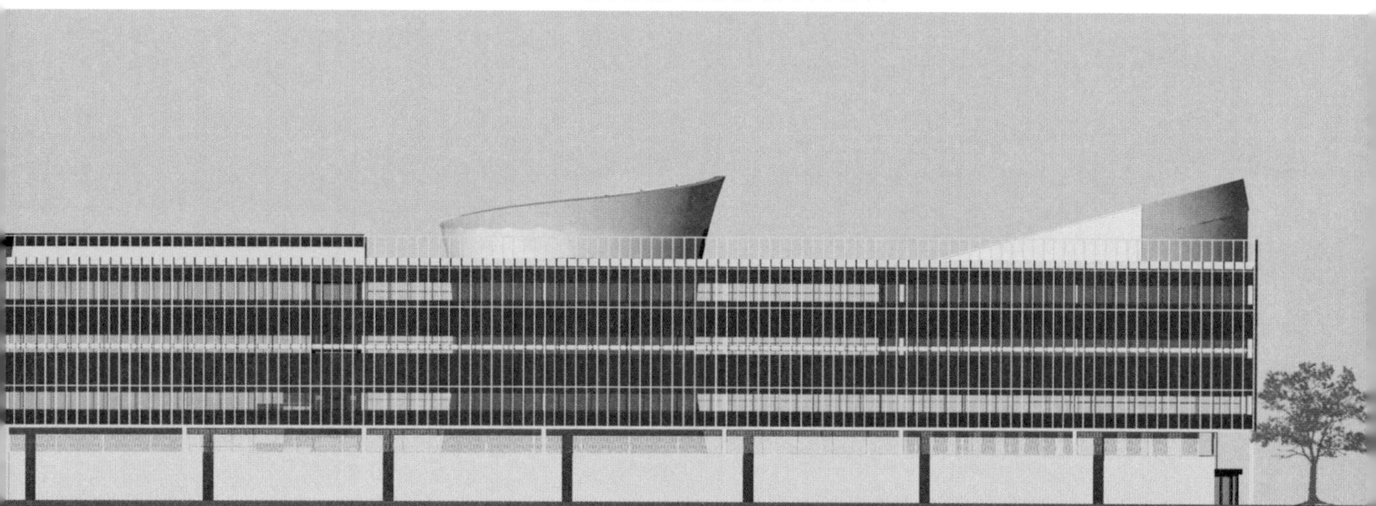

The jury consisted of a highly representative selection of magistrates, personalities chosen for their status and professional skills, all Finnish. It was assisted by a joint working group of experts around several of its members.
Six projects were selected and invited to compete in the second round. The project submitted by CS Studio Architects, called *In-between*, did not make it. The impression one gets from the inevitably partial and fragmented picture provided by the online[1] published material, is that the jury had focused its attention on the projects that neatly paid tribute to the global universe of formal architecture. With a surely bad taste, it selected six images that perfectly illustrate the following ironic twist stating that all these appearances are interchangeable at will: "same, same, but different."

The project submitted by CS Studio Architects can be seen as a regular orthogonal system dominated by a symmetrical geometric principle for the arrangement of building volumes. The elements that shape the facade however, deviate or escape from the rules. Five light wells make one think of water towers, built in concrete. They are designed to be opened at their top and thus create courtyards in summer. The presentation of the project and functional descriptions published by the authors reveal the scrupulous attention they pay to users expectations. Their movements are imagined and anticipated with great realistic detail. The sections show an interesting research for an interior climate system based on natural convection. The architects propose to bring to Helsinki their modus operandi consisting of giving room for interaction and empowerment to users and to profit from their creative energy for the final development and completion of the project. Their intention becomes concrete when they discuss the possibility of ordering ceramic mosaics from local artists, thus "describing the cultural diversity" of the city. This ingenuous and wonderful confidence could only fail against the rigid cultural codes of the Finnish construction industry, its "building designers" and top names from the cultural field.

1 http://competition.keskustakirjasto.fi/competition-entries/.

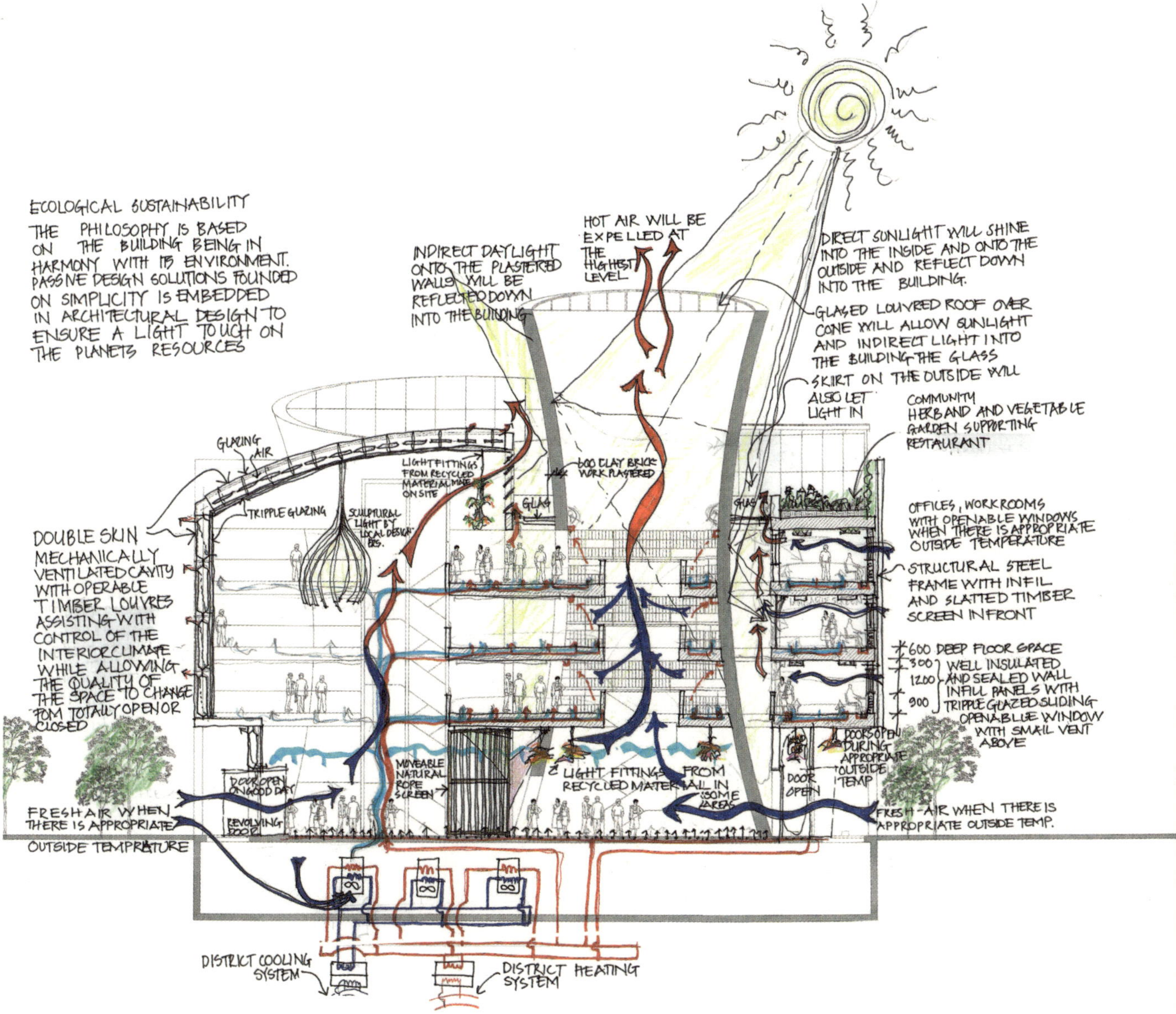

ECOLOGICAL SUSTAINABILITY
THE PHILOSOPHY IS BASED ON THE BUILDING BEING IN HARMONY WITH ITS ENVIRONMENT. PASSIVE DESIGN SOLUTIONS FOUNDED ON SIMPLICITY IS EMBEDDED IN ARCHITECTURAL DESIGN TO ENSURE A LIGHT TOUCH ON THE PLANETS RESOURCES
INDIRECT DAYLIGHT ONTO THE PLASTERED WALLS WILL BE REFLECTED DOWN INTO THE BUILDING
HOT AIR WILL BE EXPELLED AT THE HIGHEST LEVEL
DIRECT SUNLIGHT WILL SHINE INTO THE INSIDE AND ONTO THE OUTSIDE AND REFLECT DOWN INTO THE BUILDING.
GLASED LOUVRED ROOF OVER CONE WILL ALLOW SUNLIGHT AND INDIRECT LIGHT INTO THE BUILDING THE GLASS SKIRT ON THE OUTSIDE WILL ALSO LET LIGHT IN
COMMUNITY HERB AND VEGETABLE GARDEN SUPPORTING RESTAURANT
GLAZING
AIR
TRIPPLE GLAZING
SCULPTURAL LIGHT BY LOCAL DESIGNERS.
LIGHT FITTINGS FROM RECYCLED MATERIAL MADE ON SITE
600 CLAY BRICK WORK PLASTERED
GLAS
GLAS
DOUBLE SKIN MECHANICALLY VENTILATED CAVITY WITH OPERABLE TIMBER LOUVRES ASSISTING WITH CONTROL OF THE INTERIOR CLIMATE WHILE ALLOWING THE QUALITY OF THE SPACE TO CHANGE FOM TOTALLY OPEN OR CLOSED
OFFICES, WORKROOMS WITH OPENABLE WINDOWS WHEN THERE IS APPROPRIATE OUTSIDE TEMPERATURE
STRUCTURAL STEEL FRAME WITH INFIL AND SLATTED TIMBER SCREEN IN FRONT
600 DEEP FLOOR SPACE
300
1200
900
WELL INSULATED AND SEALED WALL INFILL PANELS WITH TRIPPLE GLAZED SLIDING OPENABLE WINDOW WITH SMALL VENT ABOVE
DOORS OPEN DURING APPROPRIATE OUTSIDE TEMP
DOOR OPEN
DOOR OPEN ON GOOD DAY
REVOLVING DOOR
MOVEABLE NATURAL ROPE SCREEN
LIGHT FITTINGS FROM RECYCLED MATERIAL IN SOME AREAS
FRESH AIR WHEN THERE IS APPROPRIATE OUTSIDE TEMPRATURE
FRESH-AIR WHEN THERE IS APPROPRIATE OUTSIDE TEMP.
DISTRICT COOLING SYSTEM
DISTRICT HEATING SYSTEM

PHILANI HEALTH CLINIC, UNDER THE AUSPICES OF THE INDEPENDENT DEVELOPMENT TRUST, CRADOCK, EASTERN CAPE, 1996, CS STUDIO ARCHITECTS /////////

The Independent Development Trust (IDT)[1] was created in 1990 and is funded by the South African government. It promotes the construction of social facilities needed in the domains of housing, education and health services for disadvantaged black communities. In twenty-five years it has initiated and supported nearly 8,800 projects.

The Philani Health Clinic project finds itself in a very particular context. It is largely determined by previous work and is actually ground-breaking for CS Studio Architects in Cradock.

We know the great effectiveness of relatively simple programs that allow a wide audience to access basic health care. Cuba spends less than 5 % of the health budget per capita of the United States and achieves equal results in terms of life expectancy, or even better. Between 1965 and 1975 Mao's China, with its "barefoot doctors", greatly improved the health status of its population, as testified by World Health Organization studies. The needs that the Cradock clinic had to meet were identified and defined collectively in a local committee of public health, bringing together residents of the Lingelihle community. They drafted the programme requirements, which were submitted to the IDT for approval.

The originality of this much-appreciated project lies in its housing a comprehensive care centre and a preventive medicine unit under one roof. The clinic actually consists of two symmetrical buildings facing each other, connected by a reception unit and a common waiting room. It sits on the top of a hill and gives off the impression of a kind attention to the surrounding neighbourhoods it serves. The clearly functional character of volumes and forms is rather overt. Its construction with brick walls, tin roofs and white painted window frames evoke images of Scandinavian architecture.

1
"Who We Are", Independent Development Trust: http://www.idt.org.za/who-we-are/.

DELFT SYMPHONY WAY, COMMUNITY DAY CENTRE.
DELFT, SILVERSAND MAIN ROAD/OUTENIKWA ROAD, CAPE TOWN, WESTERN CAPE, 2011-2015, EQUITY STUDIO (PTY) LTD /////////

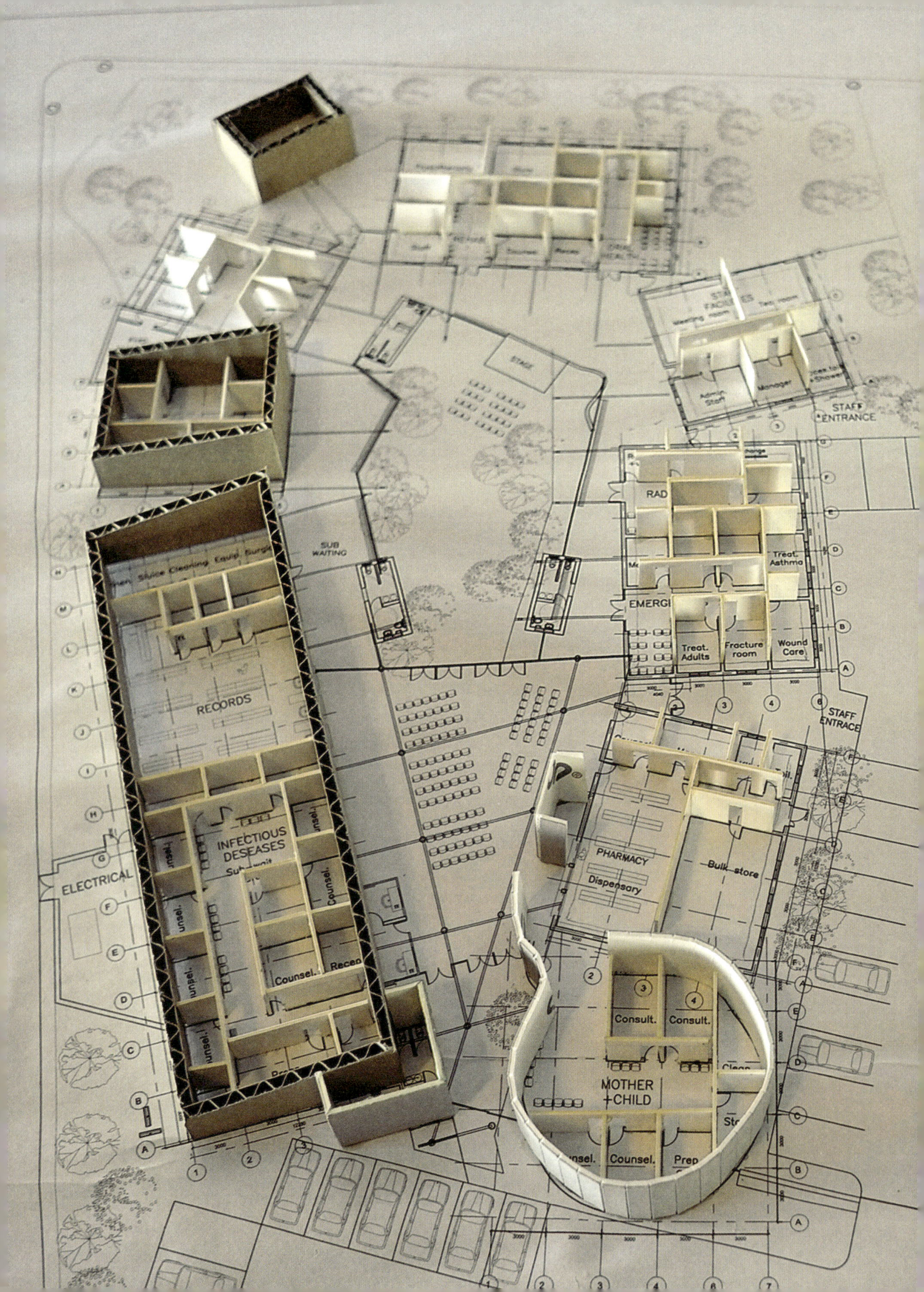
STAGE
SUB WAITING
STAFF ENTRANCE
Treat. Asthma
Treat. Adults
Fracture room
Wound Care
RECORDS
INFECTIOUS DESEASES
ELECTRICAL
PHARMACY
Dispensary
Bulk store
Consult.
Consult.
MOTHER +CHILD
Counsel.
Prep

How to build a public health facility destined to become a landmark in a still non-existent urban landscape? This was the question in the development of this clinic. It sits on a plot of 4,900 square metres located near the airport, in a developing area of which the character was unknown at the time of planning. The architects took inspiration from Fabrizio Carola's Kaedi Hospital in Mauritania, which is set up as a village hospital and tapers the interaction that is typical of its spaces, conceived in terms of healing and interdependencies between patients, their families and their relatives.

The clinic is divided into twelve distinct yet not isolated buildings, organized around a central green courtyard with an amphitheatre and connected by a closed passageway. The reception and distribution room is distinguished by its large volume and thus defines both layout and orientation. Its high visibility from the road clearly marks the ensemble. From there, visitors are directed to specialized areas dependent on their needs.

1
Equity Studio was established parallel to the CS Studio agency in order to meet the requirements of the BBBEE program (see p. 203). Equity Studio was dissolved on June 1 2016 due to bureaucratic mistakes and corruption problems related to the implementation of the programme. In practice, the CS Studio Architects have, amidst great difficulties, transferred power, knowledge and skills to their subsidiary, in accordance with the original intention of the programme.

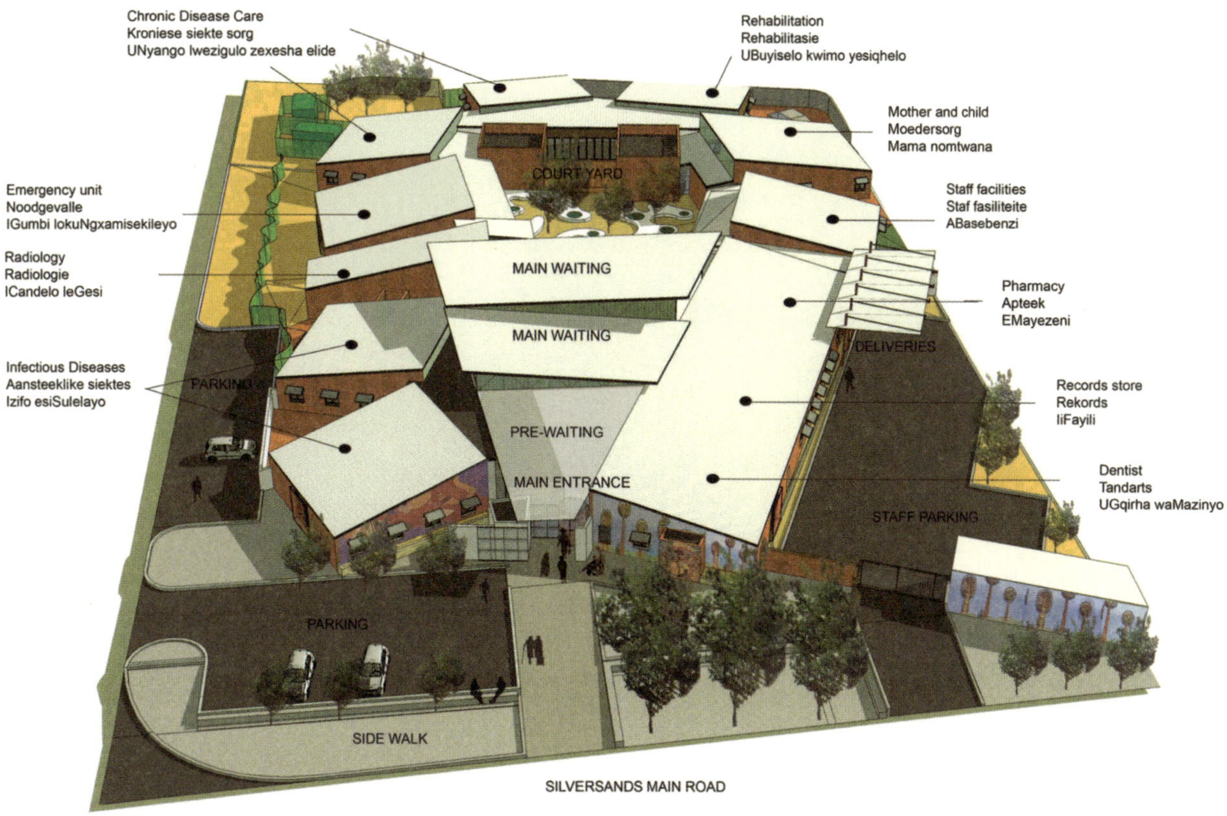

The articulation of the individual buildings creates stretches of contact on each of their sides and leaves interstices that offer a stage for recreation or specific therapeutic activities. When strolling between buildings and along the gangways, one finds views to the outside behind every corner. Through the direction of light they provide a sense of location and orientation, thus lowering the stress of visitors. This is generously applied throughout the project, but never overly abundant. Volumes, shapes, colours, views and light wells make up the architectural substance, much more than the masses, surfaces or materials could ever do.

The elaboration is simple with exposed brick walls, aluminium locks on doors and windows and sheet-metal roofing. For the architects, construction was significantly slowed down and burdened by bureaucratic procedures that in South Africa, as in the rest of the world, are "the result of the gradual fusion of public and private power into a single entity, saturated with rules and regulations".[2] On the ground, once opened, the clinic was enthusiastically received by its users, who hasten to say that they never could have imagined that a clinic could be characterized by its architecture's engaging nature. Those in charge of the project at the state office are likely to remember the atypical nature of the whole process.

2
David Graeber. *Bureaucratie.*

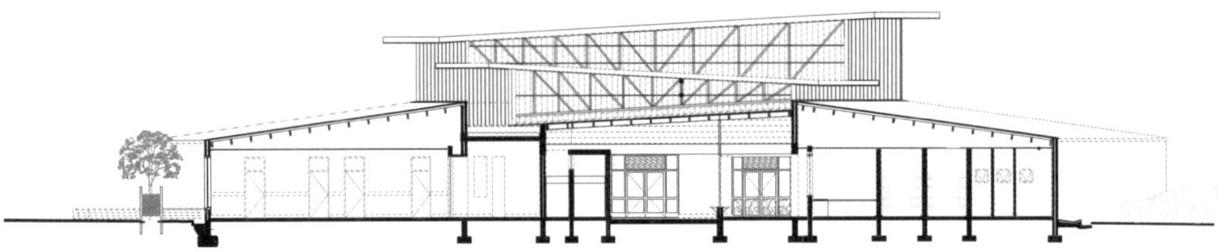

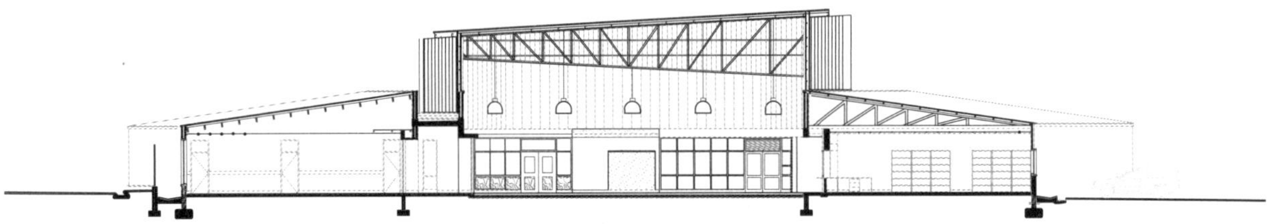

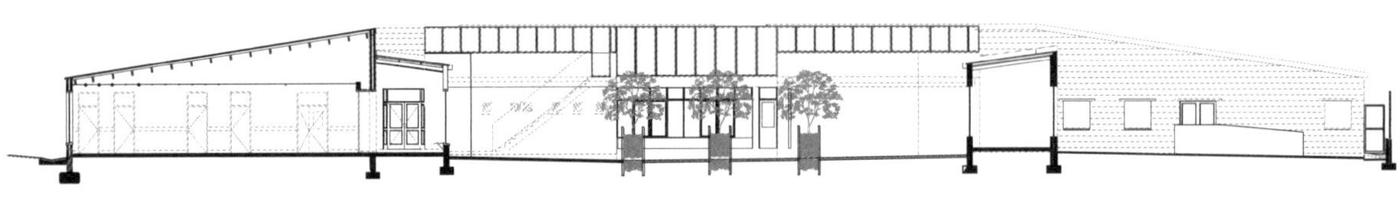

GUGA S'THEBE ARTS, CULTURE AND HERITAGE VILLAGE 1 (1996-1999) AND 2 (2006-2015), CULTURAL AND COMMUNITY CENTRE, LANGA, WESTERN CAPE, CS STUDIO ARCHITECTS

THIS ACHIEVEMENT WAS RECOGNIZED IN 2008 WITH THE GLOBAL AWARD FOR SUSTAINABLE ARCHITECTURE AND IN 2010 WITH THE DESIGN AND HEALTH INTERNATIONAL ACADEMY AWARD.
////////

"*Guga S'Thebe Kudala Usophulela*" is a Xhosa idiom praising an ageing serving platter for its enduring friendly service. The platter serves everyone welcomed into the house, and has served many generations and different types of people from all walks of life, nourishing and preparing them for the future.

The site is located on the corner of Washington and Church streets in Langa. To its east sits the site where thousands of people burnt their passes before marching to town in 1954. The building deals with the significance of the site while clearly being a public building despite its modest size. The aim of the project is to provide a home for arts, culture and heritage for the Western Cape, which is unique and culturally reflective.

This is clearly a post-apartheid building. In the first place it deals with the community's needs as the design's principle, and secondly the response is rooted on the site. The architecture is unique but generically more closely associated to the fragmentation of a squatter camp than the monotony of the Apartheid Township.

"The building is only 820 square metres in total but includes four artists' studios, two of which will be used for performing arts and two for visual arts. The 'cone' space is designed to be an events and visual arts multipurpose space which makes reference to the traditional 'rondawel' vernacular. For small intimate performances it is able to host 150 spectators. The outdoor stage and seating is used for bigger performances."[1]

With more than 300,000 visitors per year, this community centre has developed to what is now a sight-seeing destination in the tour operators' repertoire. It has become a kind of alternative global icon, which is all the more reason for describing it on the official CS Studio Architects website. Especially because the increasing success asks for more contact with the global architectural scene; it obliges clarification and critical interrogation.

CS Studio Architects places Guga S'Thebe clearly in the range of post-apartheid achievements since it is strictly in relation to the needs and agenda of local communities; it is grouped in the oldest township in the Cape Town region. However, the ensemble's shape relates more to the slums than to the uniformity of the township. The project process, which lasted eighteen months, allowed the consideration of several plan- and form-generating principles. All were discussed around scale models. They enabled the requests of the elders to be granted, to group the buildings around a rondavel,[2] while the young were already focused on sports cars and information technology. The town's architectural principle is based on circulation patterns that were already present on the site and that could be mapped with aerial photography. The result was a kind of village in which interstices and circulation provide the "holds" for the unfolding of contacts and social interaction. The many visual elements of colourful ceramics allowed community members to learn forms of artistic expression.

1
http://csstudio.co.za/Guga%20Stebi1.html

2
Circular hut, typical of southern Africa.

The site was subject to strict conditions in terms of the geography of the origin of materials (30 kilometres unless absolutely necessary) or that of the workforce being both trained and employed on site (resident within a radius of three kilometres).

The second step was planned and sanitaires et de restauration) developed as part of events organized for the designation of Cape Town as World Design Capital. On a site located behind the centre, a consortium of stakeholders aggregated around CS Studio Architects including the Peter Behrens School of Architecture (Düsseldorf), the School of Architecture of the University of Aachen and the Georgia Institute of Technology (Atlanta)[3] undertook the development, planning, financing and building of a theatre and its complementary facilities (control room, recording studio, sanitation and restoration). Financing deserves special mention; it was the German magazine *AIT* who assured it after the patient efforts of its readers for over ten years. It is remarkable that students and teachers have kindly provided the project elements and their implementation on the site, and that they have personally funded their travel and the expenses for their stay. As photographs prove, the site really consisted of transposition to the 1:1 scale of elements studied in models representing the simultaneous geometrical arrangement of materials and techniques. At the centre of international debates, it allowed generalization, exchange and transfer in all technical directions through dealing with recovery of materials or entire building elements and the implementation of newly "rediscovered", explored and systematically studied techniques.[4]

For CS Studio Architects, the site of this second phase represented a rich opportunity for exchange, while at the same time they were solicited to remove the many sources of disturbance. The contribution of the agency was limited to the formulation of the master plan and the general principle; subsequent decisions and implementation of details were the responsibility of the visiting architecture professors. The general impression is that the atmosphere of a "good-will mission" is tangible.

3
Design, Develop, Build: http://www.designdevelopbuild.com/.

4
In particular insulation elements made of light loam. On this subject see Franz Volhard, *Construire en terre allégée*, Arles: Actes Sud, 2016; or Franz Volhard, *Bauen Mit Leichtlehm: Handbuch Für Das Bauen Mit Holz Und Lehm*, Basel: Birkhäuser Verlag GmbH, 2015.

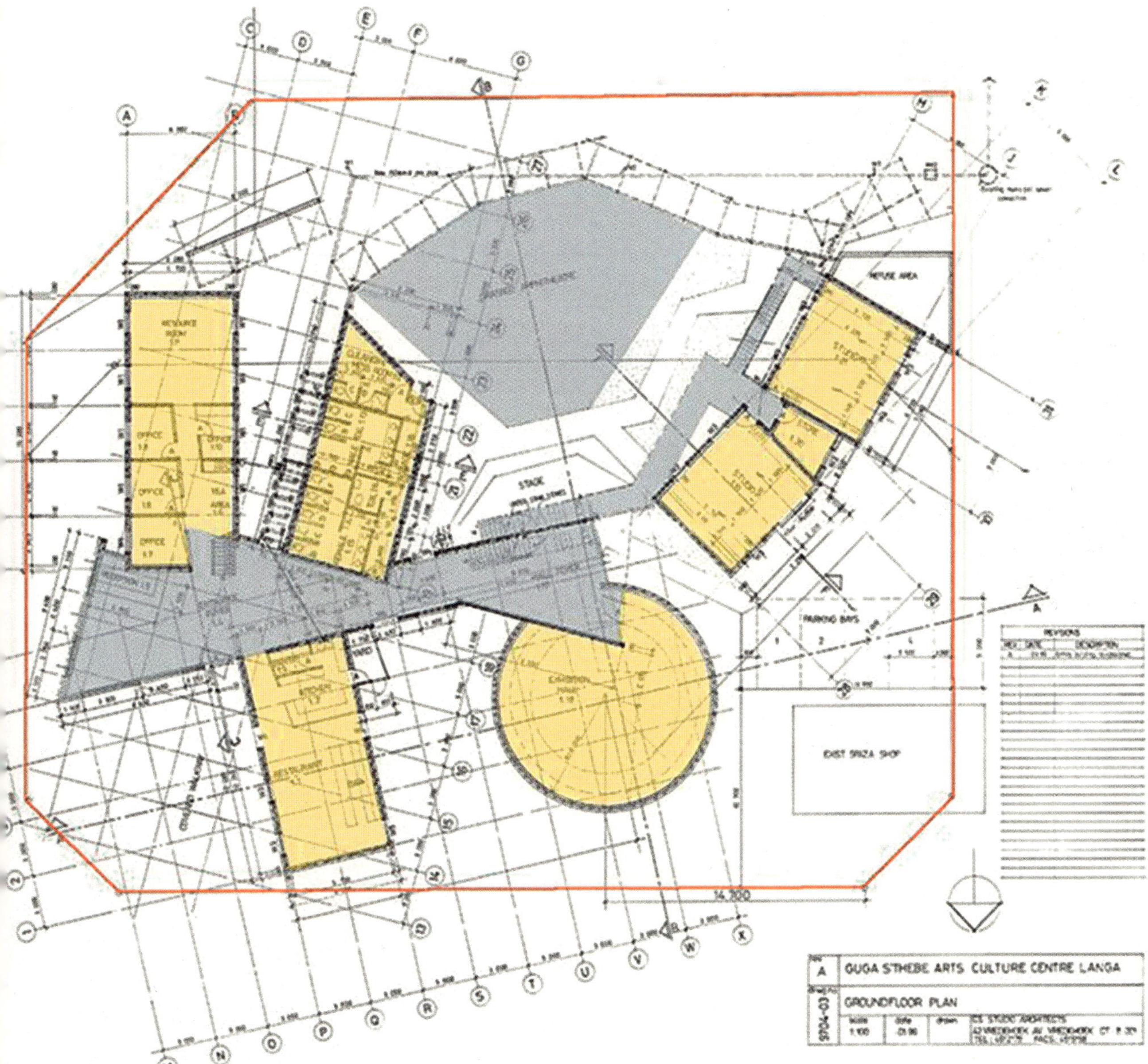

GUGA S'THEBE ARTS CULTURE CENTRE LANGA
GROUNDFLOOR PLAN
STAGE
PARKING BAYS
EXIST SPAZA SHOP
REFUSE AREA
REVISIONS
14.700

DIE NEELSIE, ARBEIDSGENOT, HOME OF
C. J. LANGENHOVEN, OUDTSHOORN, WESTERN CAPE, 2006-2008
CS STUDIO ARCHITECTS ////////

Die Neelsie

Since 1994 Afrikaans is one of the ten official languages of the Republic of South Africa.[2] Although the post-apartheid period quite logically has seen its influence decline insofar as the ruling party, the African National Congress (ANC) makes use of the local languages and English, it has emerged as one of the multi-ethnic languages due to its place among Coloured people (mixed are about 3.4 million people, against 2.7 million whites).[3] As such, Afrikaans basically descends from Dutch. Its own theoretical foundations were developed in at least two significant steps, the first in 1875 under the aegis of S. J. du Toit, who worked especially on publishing a patriotic magazine in Afrikaans and who campaigned for the recognition of the historical language alongside English. The second step was made by Cornelis Jacobus Langenhoven, a lawyer born in 1873 and committed to the promotion of Afrikaans instead of Dutch. He worked on structuring its use and enriching its vocabulary by introducing neologisms. His contribution was decisive for the creolization of the language and its dissemination.

This project's intervention consisted of entrusting to CS Studio Architects the creation of a cultural facility on the property of late C. J. Langenhoven; while a colleague was in charge of a very conservative restoration of the mansion. The programme may seem somewhat paradoxical, with its intention to establish a centre where cultures should blend on a fetish historic site of only one of them. As for the rest, numerous bureaucratic complications followed each other, some up to the minister in charge.

CS Studio Architects began by addressing the programme with a landscape architecture proposal consisting of a small open-air amphitheatre south-west of the house. The proposal met with persistent opposition from neighbours, fed by it seems old discordant relationships on this site. By convention, the property was eventually divided into three areas: a narrow band south for the construction of a multipurpose building including theatre, meeting room and exhibition area. Near the property line it hosts, as if under its wing, a small service building. It was literally about installing "an empty box in which each could bring the cultural project he held close to his heart".[4] With this building, CS Studio Architects made its mark with an extremely refined and efficient achievement, true to the original principles of its architecture but expressing a talent now at its top. The reception, circulation, workplaces and exhibition spaces are nested, versatile and almost interchangeable. Light seems literally constructed here. On the outside, the elementary volume of this regular parallelepiped is defined by a front wall that widely stretches out; it is accompanied by a cornice over the full length, connecting it with the garden wall and thus forming an entrance porch. The geometry of the ensemble allows one to experience the created perspective, even better than the approach from the Langenhoven home-museum does with its narrow angle of less than 30 degrees. Inside, the volumes are placed along

1
J. M. Coetzee, *Boyhood: Scenes from Provincial Life*, London: Penguin, 1998, 125.

2
English, Afrikaans, Zulu, Xhosa, Tswana, Northern Sotho, Venda, Tsonga, Swati and Transvaal Ndebele.

3
In South Africa the term Coloured refers to a distinct ethnic group, predominantly made up of people of mixed race.

4
Interview with Carin Smuts by the author, 5 January 2016.

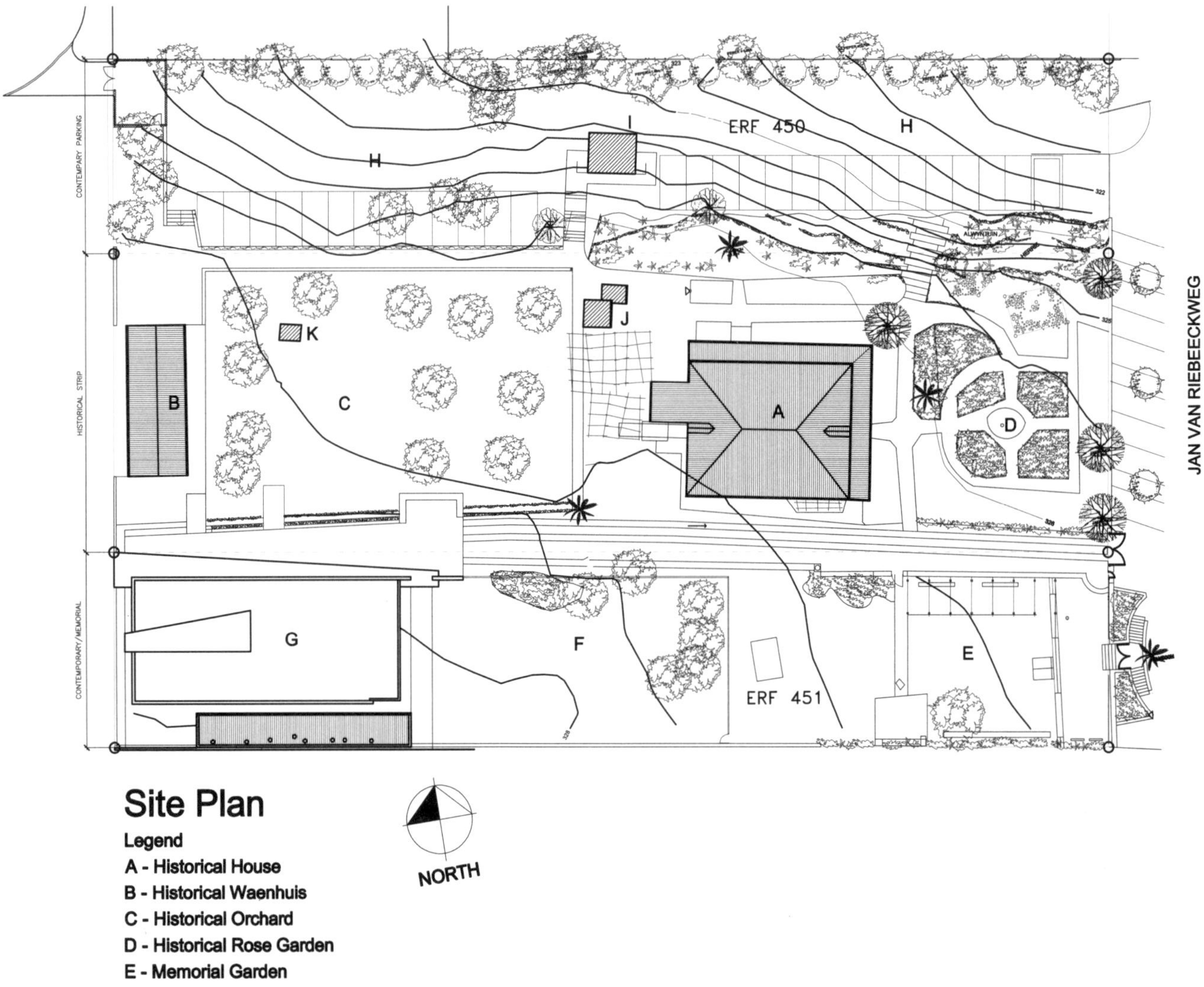

Site Plan

Legend

A - Historical House
B - Historical Waenhuis
C - Historical Orchard
D - Historical Rose Garden
E - Memorial Garden
F - Outside Seating Area
G -Die Neelsie
H - Parking
I - Ablution and Information
J - Existing Toilets
K - Existing Chicken shed

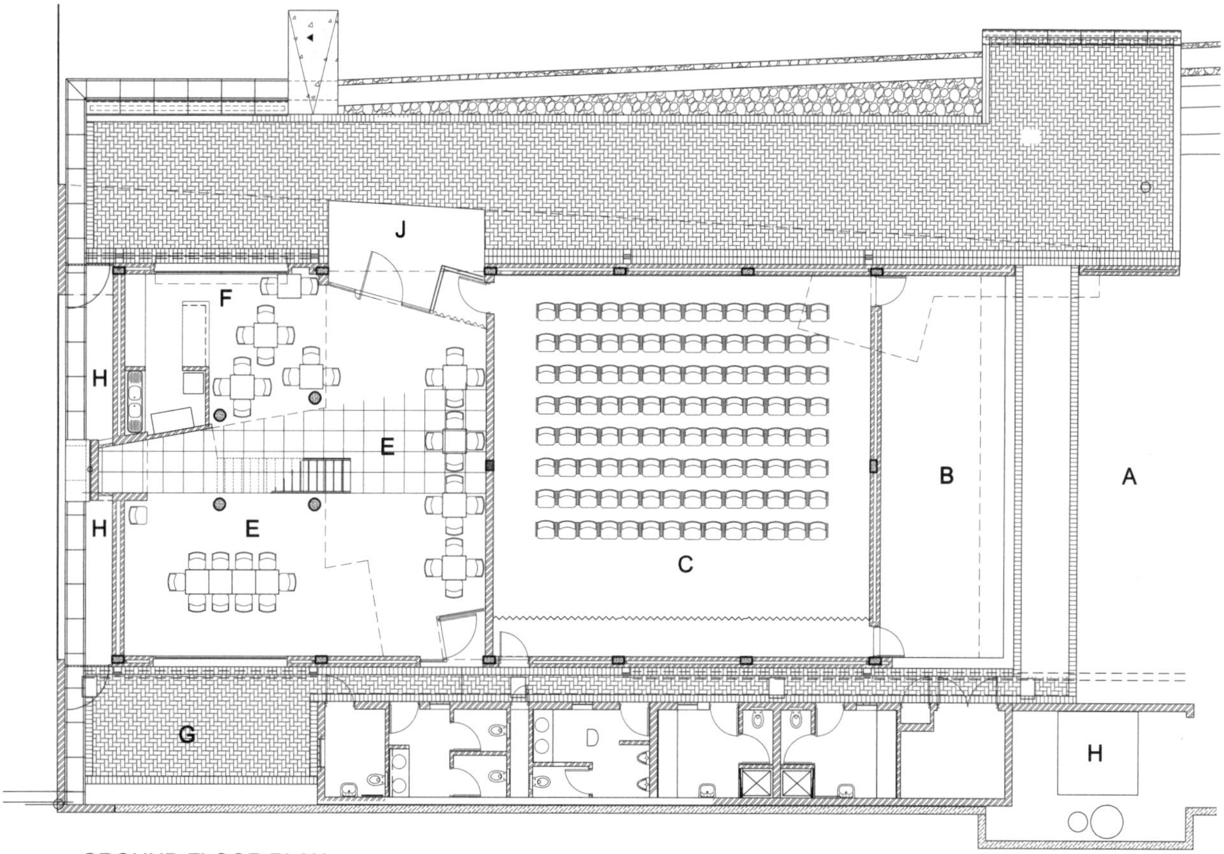

GROUND FLOOR PLAN

Legend
A - Outdoor Seating Area
B - Outdoor Stage Area
C - Multi-Purpose Theatre
D - Ablution block
E - Foyer/Exibition
F - Restuarant
G - Courtyard
H - AC/Service yard
J - Stoep and entrance

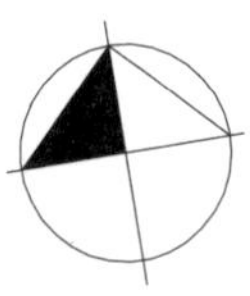

irregular angles, distinguishing the spaces without characterizing them too specifically, creating zones for exchange, circulation and activity. The building hosts a courtyard balcony as control room and allows the use of the outside space as a second stage, with the facade as scenery. The materials express a Finnish functionalism implemented with great care and mastery of surfaces and colours.

***"When he speaks Afrikaans
all the complications of life seem
suddenly to fall away.
Afrikaans is like a ghostly envelope that
accompanies him everywhere,
that he is free to slip into,
becoming at once another person,
simpler, gayer, lighter in his tread."***

— J. M. Coetzee, *Boyhood: Scenes from Provincial Life.*

ULWAZI YOUTH CENTRE, PHASES 1 AND 2, LANGA, CAPE TOWN, WESTERN CAPE, 1989–1998: CONSTRUCTION. NOVEMBER 2009: DESTRUCTION BY ORGANIZED VANDALISM, CS STUDIO ARCHITECTS

In each of CS Studio Architects' community construction sites, techniques and building materials are chosen with the intention of creating maximum employment opportunities for an under-qualified workforce suffering endemic unemployment. This way of working has positive effects on three levels: it stimulates the flow of money in the local economy sustained by the created demand; it gives employees their dignity and allows them to acquire new experiences; finally it avoids the use of credit and its subsequent dependence and corruption. This process helps to materialize the collective, material, formal and symbolic appropriation of the building by its builders and users. It is the foundation of social control over the building.

The opportunities created by the recyclable materials market did not escape the attention of mafioso criminal organizations and South African gangs. They mobilized henchmen who devoted several days to the systematic demolition of the Ulwazi Centre in order to sell the materials on the recycling market. The fact that a local contractor equipped to practice the orthodoxy of reinforced concrete construction, immediately after this happening, proposed to rebuild the whole thing speaks volumes about the circles that mainstream materials allow to grease and grow.

By laying a criminal hand on this facility built by the will of a community eager to emancipate its youth from the grip of gangs, publicans and shebeens, organized crime took possession of both an instrument and process of emancipation. Ulwazi Centre was intended as a facility for a particularly disenfranchised neighbourhood, originally established to provide the city of Cape Town with abundant and cheap labour. The dwellings made of hostels,[2] houses, and huts where sometimes up to twenty-four people were sharing a room, did not receive any kind of public facility.

The building, set on a plot of 1,061 square metres, was built around a raised and transformed hostel and spread out to form a courtyard, an essential protected place. School classes were included; in a second stage a kindergarten and a primary school were added. At the time of the criminal destruction, it provided classroom space for 1,300 children. The evil nature of this act of vandalism in 2009 is particularly profound because it attacks not only the final result but the very emancipating process of building a vital community facility.

1
J. M. Coetzee, *Age of Iron*, London: Penguin, 1990.

2
A sort of home where migrant workers can rent rooms or beds and access minimal infrastructure (sanitary etc.).

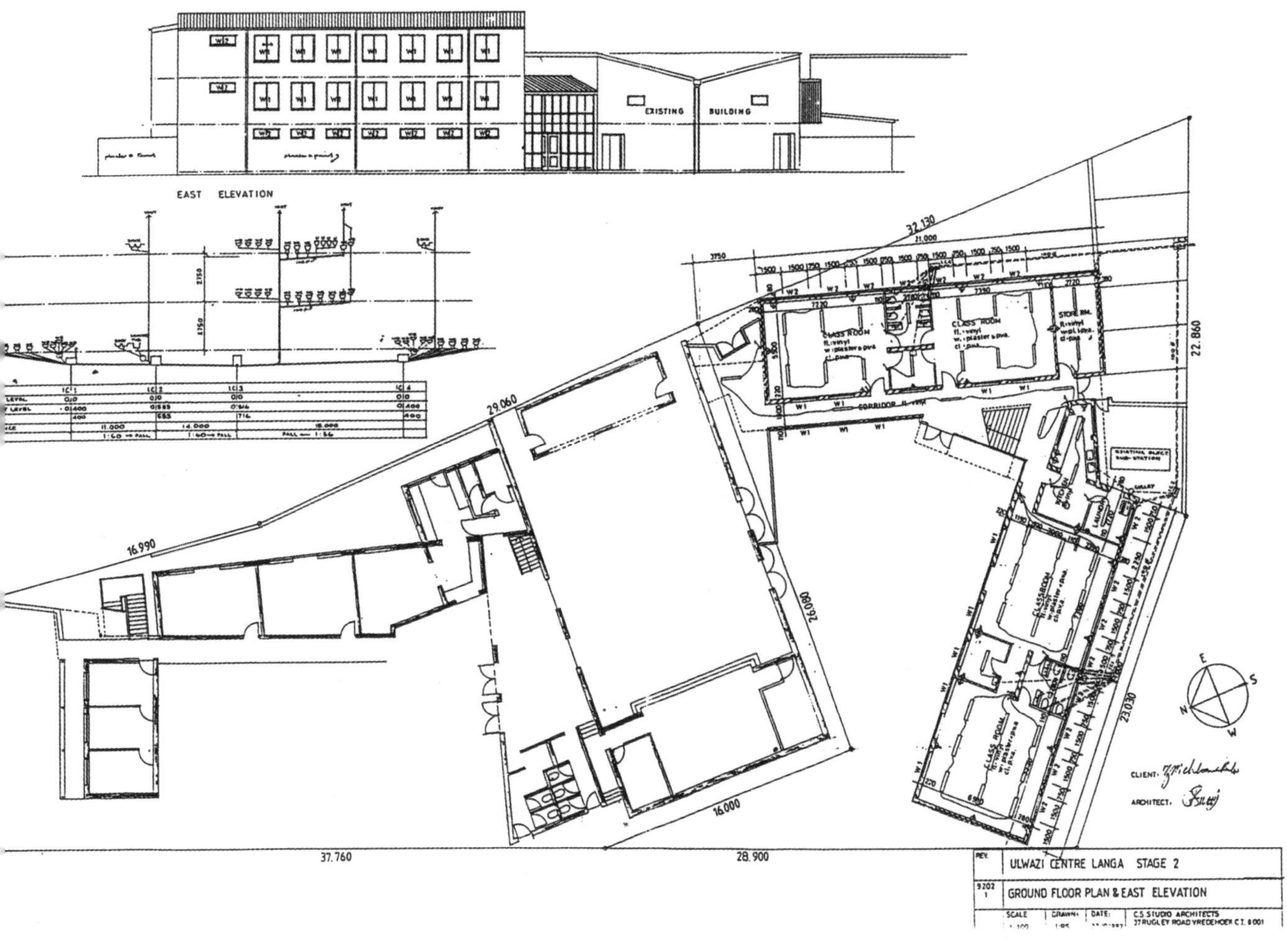
EAST ELEVATION
EXISTING BUILDING
CLASS ROOM
STORE RM.
CORRIDOR
CLASSROOM
CLASS ROOM
CLIENT.
ARCHITECT.
ULWAZI CENTRE LANGA STAGE 2
GROUND FLOOR PLAN & EAST ELEVATION
SCALE
DRAWN
DATE:
C.S. STUDIO ARCHITECTS
37.760
28.900
16.000
29.060
16.990
26.080
23.030
22.860
32.130

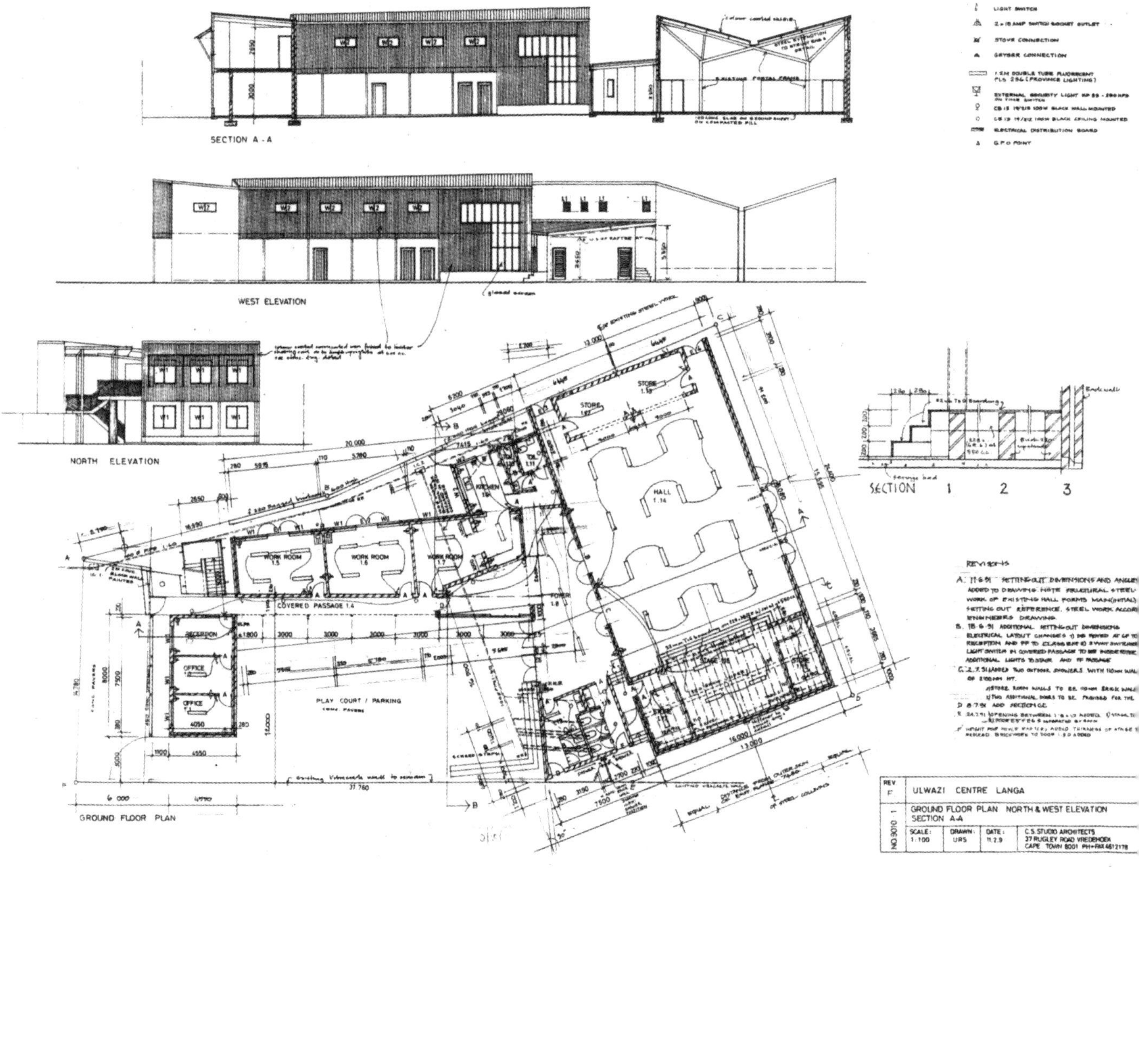
SECTION A - A
WEST ELEVATION
NORTH ELEVATION
GROUND FLOOR PLAN
WORK ROOM 1.5
WORK ROOM 1.6
KITCHEN
HALL 1.14
STORE
COVERED PASSAGE 1.4
RECEPTION
OFFICE
OFFICE
PLAY COURT / PARKING
SECTION 1 2 3
REVISIONS
ULWAZI CENTRE LANGA
GROUND FLOOR PLAN NORTH & WEST ELEVATION
SECTION A-A
SCALE: 1:100
DRAWN: URS
DATE: 11.2.9
C.S. STUDIO ARCHITECTS
37 RUGLEY ROAD VREDEHOEK
CAPE TOWN 8001 PH+FAX 4612178

"You told me
you admire your son's generation
because they are afraid of nothing.
Be careful: they may start by being careless of
their own lives and
end by being careless of everyone else's.
What you admire in them
is not necessarily what is best."

— J. M. Coetzee, *Age of Iron*.

WESBANK MULTIPURPOSE CENTRE,
DELFT, KUILS RIVER, WESTERN CAPE, 2007-2008,
CS STUDIO ARCHITECTS /////////

The need for this facility emerged in the course of the school's planning period.[1] In response to an extreme rise in violence and crime, characteristic of the disintegration that affected black communities after 1990, whereas they used to be paradoxically united by the discriminatory policy of apartheid. The planning of this project, conducted with the help of a systematic use of models, involved more than 450 people and enabled a programme comprising a multi-purpose community building, a clinic and a taxi rank. The bureaucratic procedures of permits and fundraising for this facility spanned more than seven years of bitter struggle.

The space came into being following the same DNA as the agency's other achievements; it consists of modestly dimensioned buildings grouped around courtyards, connected by corridors and passageways maximizing efficacy and use. The limited budget led to the use of large exposed bricks. This restriction had surprisingly positive effects; the energy performance of the walls is improved by the arrangement of the masonry, maintenance in the long term is easier, and the structures appear larger.

In the context of this commission CS Studio Architects conducted planning studies for other development projects in the area.

1
See pp. 69-70.

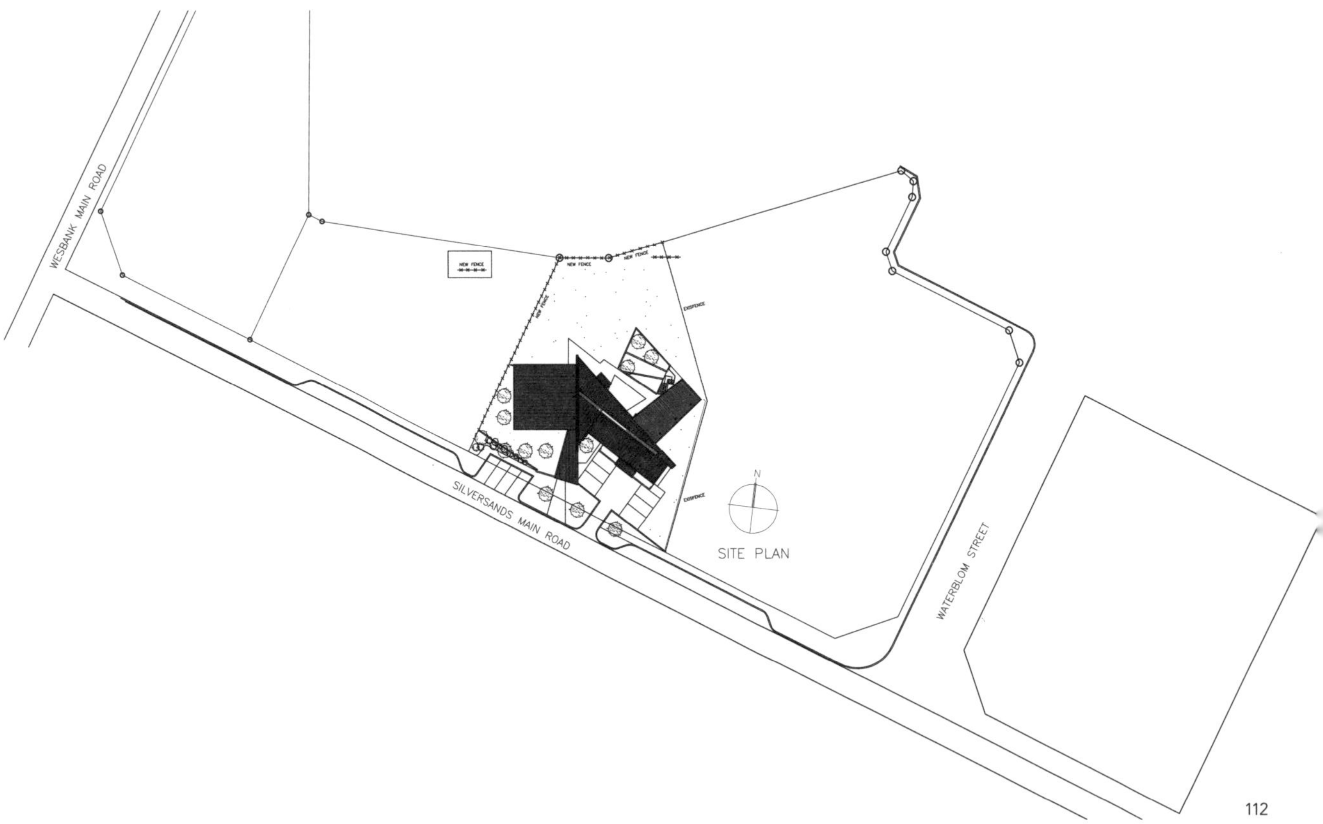

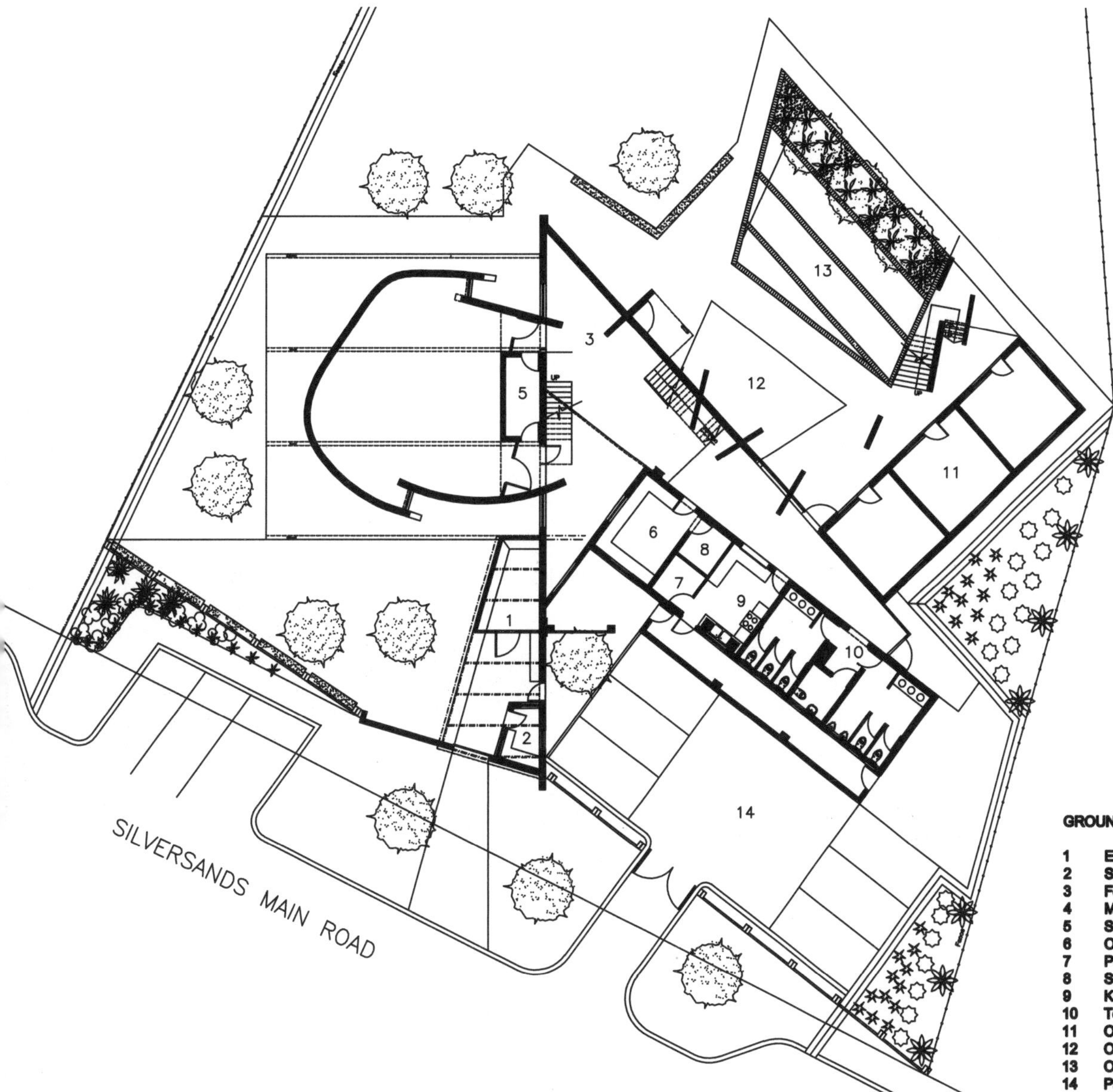

GROUND FLOOR

1 Entrance lobby
2 Security office
3 Foyer
4 Multi purpose hall
5 Store
6 Office
7 Pantry
8 Store
9 Kitchen
10 Toilets
11 Offices
12 Outdoor stage
13 Outdoor terrace
14 Parking

DAWID KLAASTE MULTIPURPOSE CENTRE, LAINGSBURG, WESTERN CAPE, 2002-2005, CS STUDIO ARCHITECTS ////////

A description of this project could begin with all the characteristics that are so typical of the agency: community initiative, recycling of materials, the decision-making process and training the workforce. But its ability to dream goes above all these considerations, as the reader can clearly see in detail in the other examples in this book and online.[1]

The Karoo, a Khoikhoi word meaning "Land of Thirst", is this semi-desert landscape that characterizes large areas in Cape Province. The road runs through vast plains with widely dispersed windmills for watering sheep. Laingsburg, 280 kilometres from Cape Town on the N1, is a small agricultural town established in the nineteenth century. The multipurpose centre is built on a plot in a "non-white" residential area, which gives it its historical and memorial significance. Otherwise, the area is renowned for its rich fauna and flora, and is famous for the discovery of a very rare specimen of a fossil eurypterid (water scorpion).

But the imagination of the local residents, of whom one assumes they are there just by default, is dominated by the railway line and especially by a dramatic flood that occurred in 1981. It still brings back memories of red rolling waters sweeping everything in their path like a herd of raging buffalos. The disaster had an enormous impact and was exacerbated by racial discrimination; government aid sent there reached only white people, leaving black people to their fate. These elements add to the symbolism of the community centre; poet Diana Ferrus, famous for her written tribute to Saartjie Baartman *I've Come to Take You Home*,[2] wrote a poem in memory of the flood's victims. The centre's building, loaded with all these emotions, has been a memorial from its very beginning. It was to be topped by a giant windmill fuelling the debate as to whether the proposed size would not tear it from its base. A railway wagon houses a restaurant and the ensemble is red, recalling the colour of the flood.

1
Sustainable by Design 2050: http://www.sbd2050.org/project/laingsburg-multi-purpose-centre-51/.

2
"South Africa Diana Ferrus: 'I've come to take you home' Tribute to Sarah Bartmann", YouTube video, 2:16, posted 14 February 2014, https://www.youtube.com/watch?v=-pCmu4uyj5c.

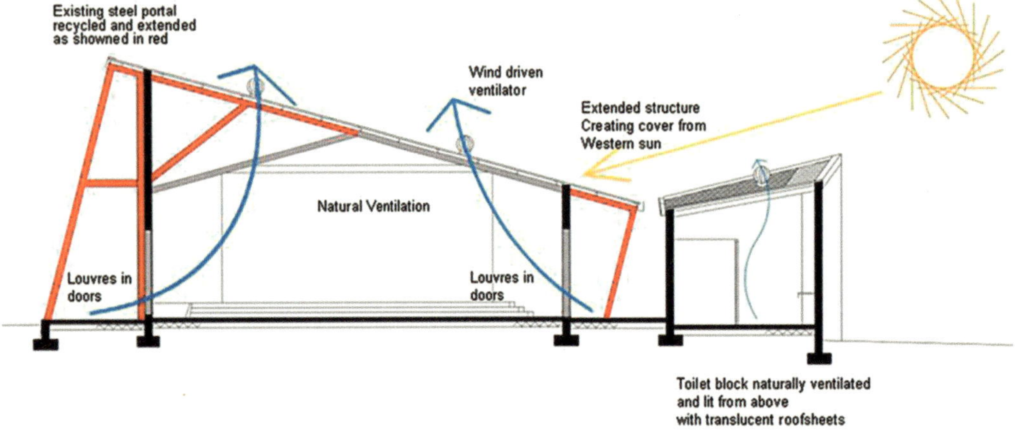

Part of the local workforce received training in welding, which allowed artist Willie Bester to coach these providential workers, teaching his techniques through internships, and train them in the construction of a decorative ensemble made of scrap recovered from the surrounding farms, giving the whole a unique and dramatic atmosphere.

In Laingsburg we find the motif of the access ramp that will be picked up and developed elsewhere, as well as the richness of nested volumes and colours characterizing spaces and forms. In 2016 a ceremony at the city cemetery should help make worthy graves for all the black people who died and who for centuries were buried in a hurry.

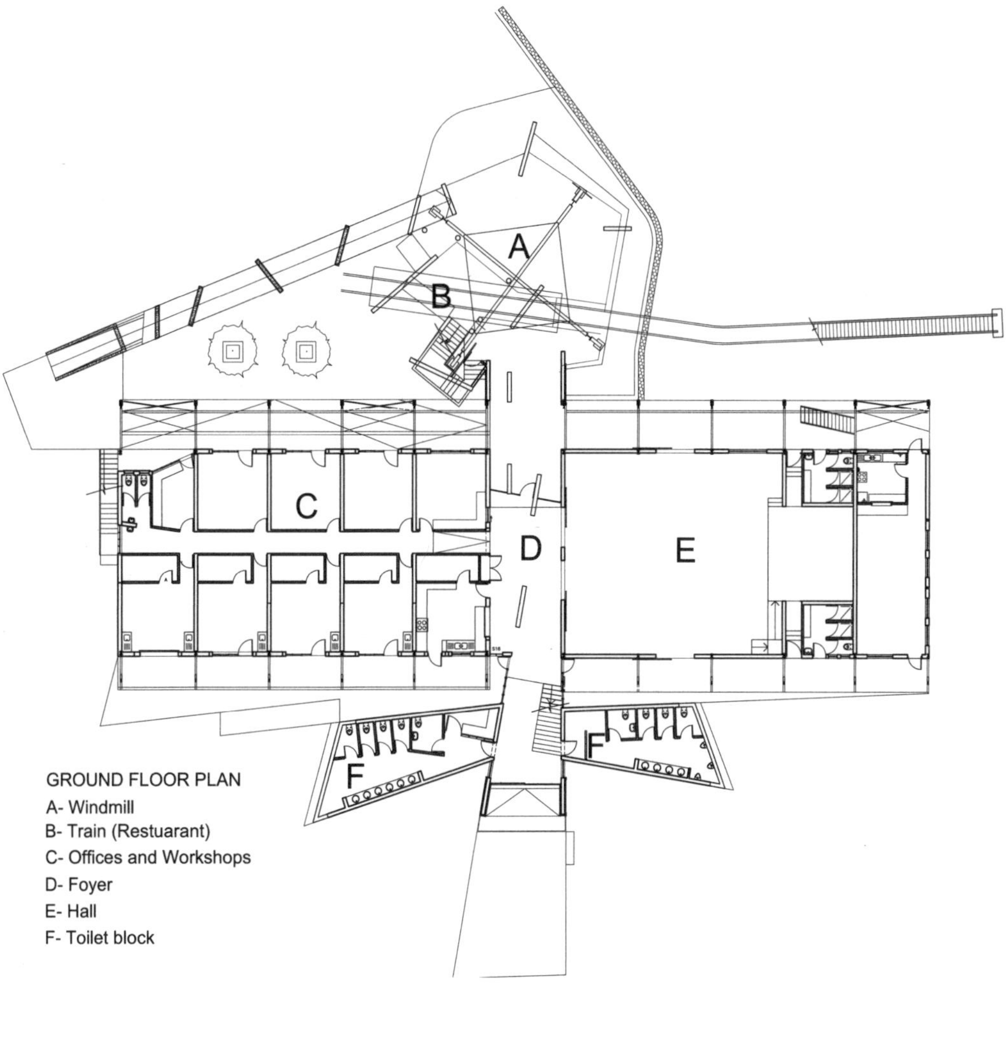

UNOBUNTU MULTIPURPOSE CULTURAL CENTRE,
WORCESTER, WESTERN CAPE,
1990-1998, CS STUDIO ARCHITECTS /////////

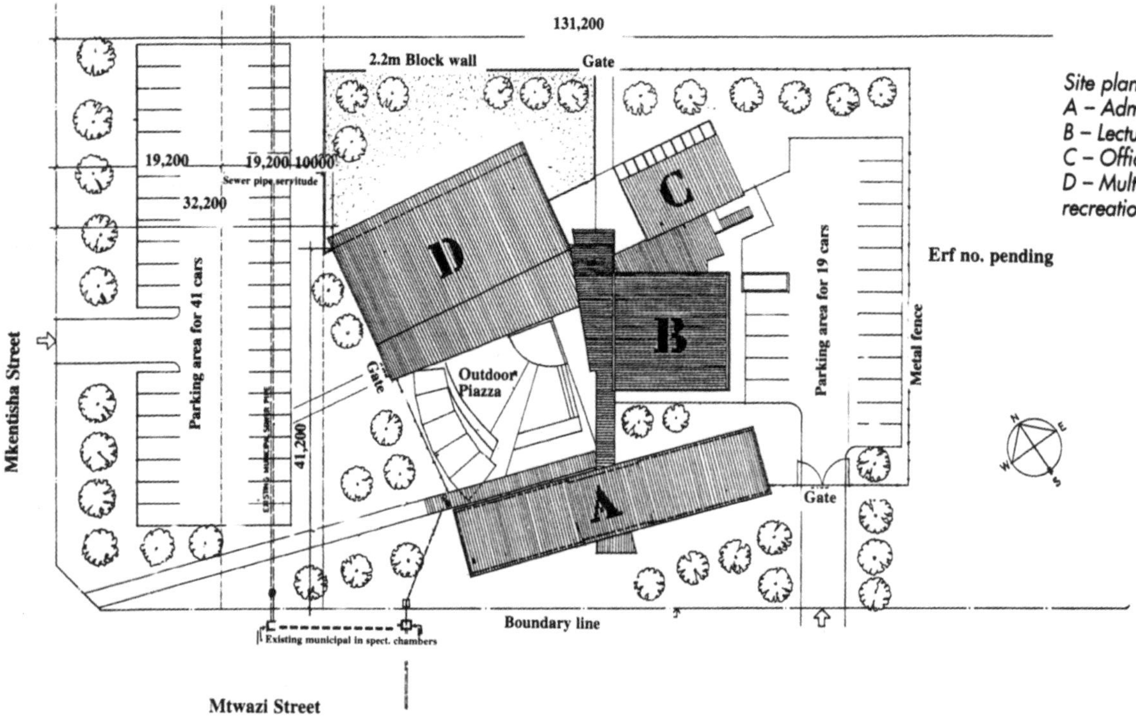

Site plan
A – Administration
B – Lecture hall
C – Offices and seminar room
D – Multi-purpose, sports and recreation hall

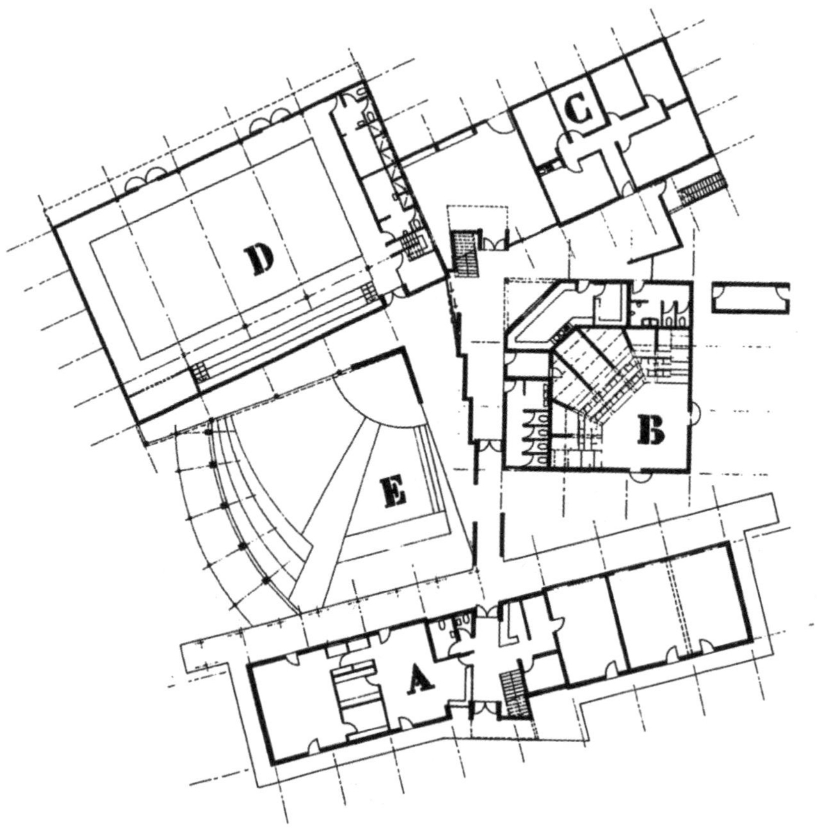

Ground floor plan
A – Admin
B – Lecture hall
C – Offices/seminar rooms
D – Multi-purpose hall
E – Outdoor amphi theatre

This project is linked to the measures taken after 1994, following a political initiative of the new authorities, the Reconstruction and Development Programme (RDP), intended to provide social facilities to historically disadvantaged communities. Another aspect of these facilities was to symbolize the existence of a civic public domain on the local scale. As part of this programme, CS Studio Architects was commissioned to establish a programme of requirements and standards for the establishment of such centres, with Unobuntu being the pilot.

The first public meetings focused on the question of where the centre should be established, i.e. on the territory of which community. Since the most pressing needs were those of the black population, it was decided to establish the centre on the site of Zweletemba. This offered various implementation alternatives; the final location was the subject of wide public debate in which the community held the authority. The project's process was managed by a representative committee elected from all local groups and organizations, which worked closely with the architects. The iterative character required the representatives to report to their constituents in all stages of the process and all decisions had to be duly validated by them.

The spatial organization is defined by four buildings creating a large protected interior area. The use of brick, metal trusses and steel cladding is both low cost and effective. Colours and protruding volumes give it a strong identity. A special feature in this ensemble was the users' request to equip it with a genuine amphitheatre "just like the university". This request was granted and it soon generated demand, so much so that surrounding white farmers now appreciate this facility in the middle of a neighbourhood once reserved for blacks.

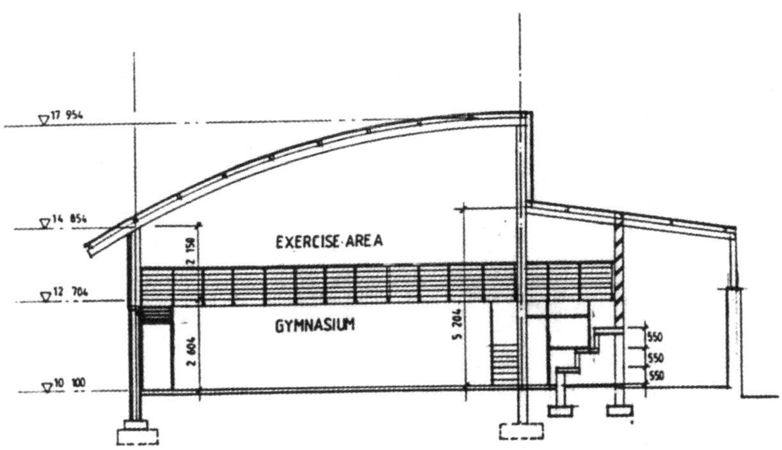

SECTION D-D

EERSTE TREETJIES (FIRST STEPS) COMMUNITY CENTRE, KOMAGGAS, NAMAQUALAND, NORTHERN CAPE, 1986–1990, CS STUDIO ARCHITECTS /////////

Komaggas is a rural village of 3,000 inhabitants in an arid area prone to periodic flooding, 100 kilometres from the nearest town, Springok, Northern Cape. At the time of the community centre's construction, employment in the region was provided by agriculture and the Kleinzee diamond mine, some 60 kilometres away.

After lengthy negotiations with an association of local community delegates, the programme covers a crèche, a library, and workshops for training and courses. The association owns the land, has funded the construction and ensures the ensemble's autonomous maintenance. The community, very attached to traditional forms of vernacular architecture (shepherd huts built of branches and covered with animal skins), wished to hold on to those forms; tradition as symbolic form thus structures this facility. The construction of steel trusses and cinderblock masonry makes use of large eaves to provide shelter and protection. Great care was given to natural ventilation and roof lights: the sheds are open on the south, as the hemisphere obliges. The construction site employed ten marginal persons considered unemployable by the diamond mine.

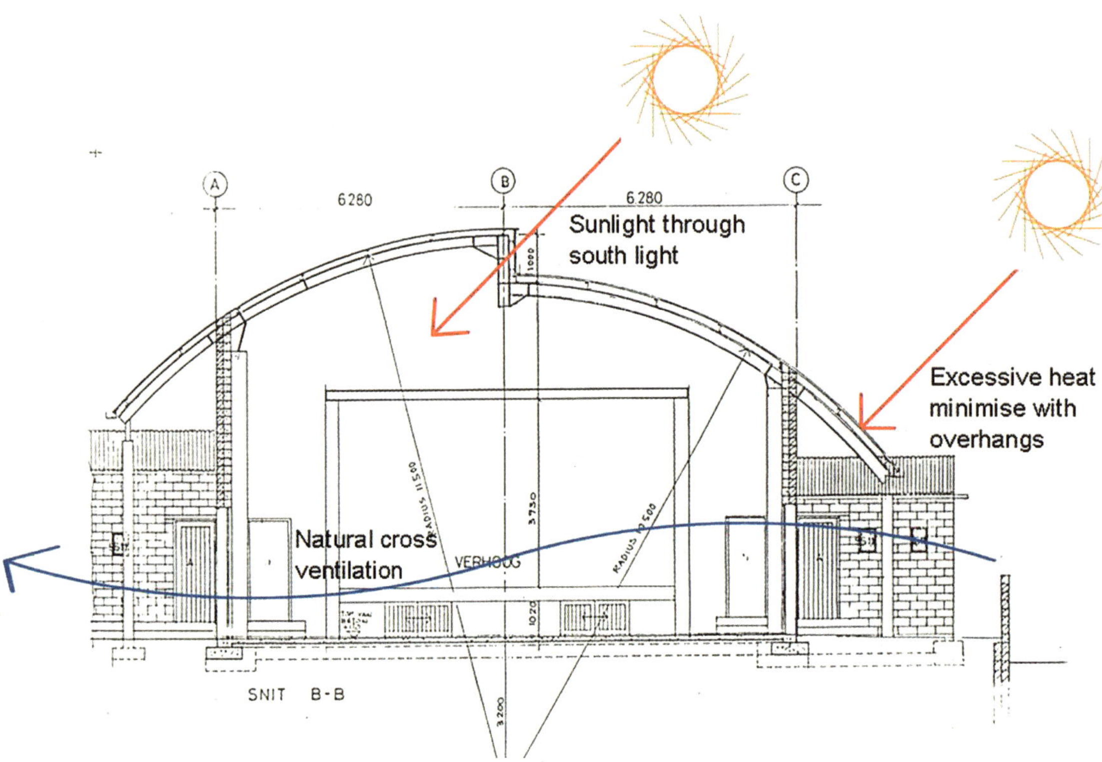

KOMAGGAS
BEVAARSKOOL&GEMEENSKAP SENTRUM
EERSTE TREETJIES

KOMAGGAS
BEVAARSKOOL&GEMEENSKAP SENTRUM
EERSTE TREETJIES

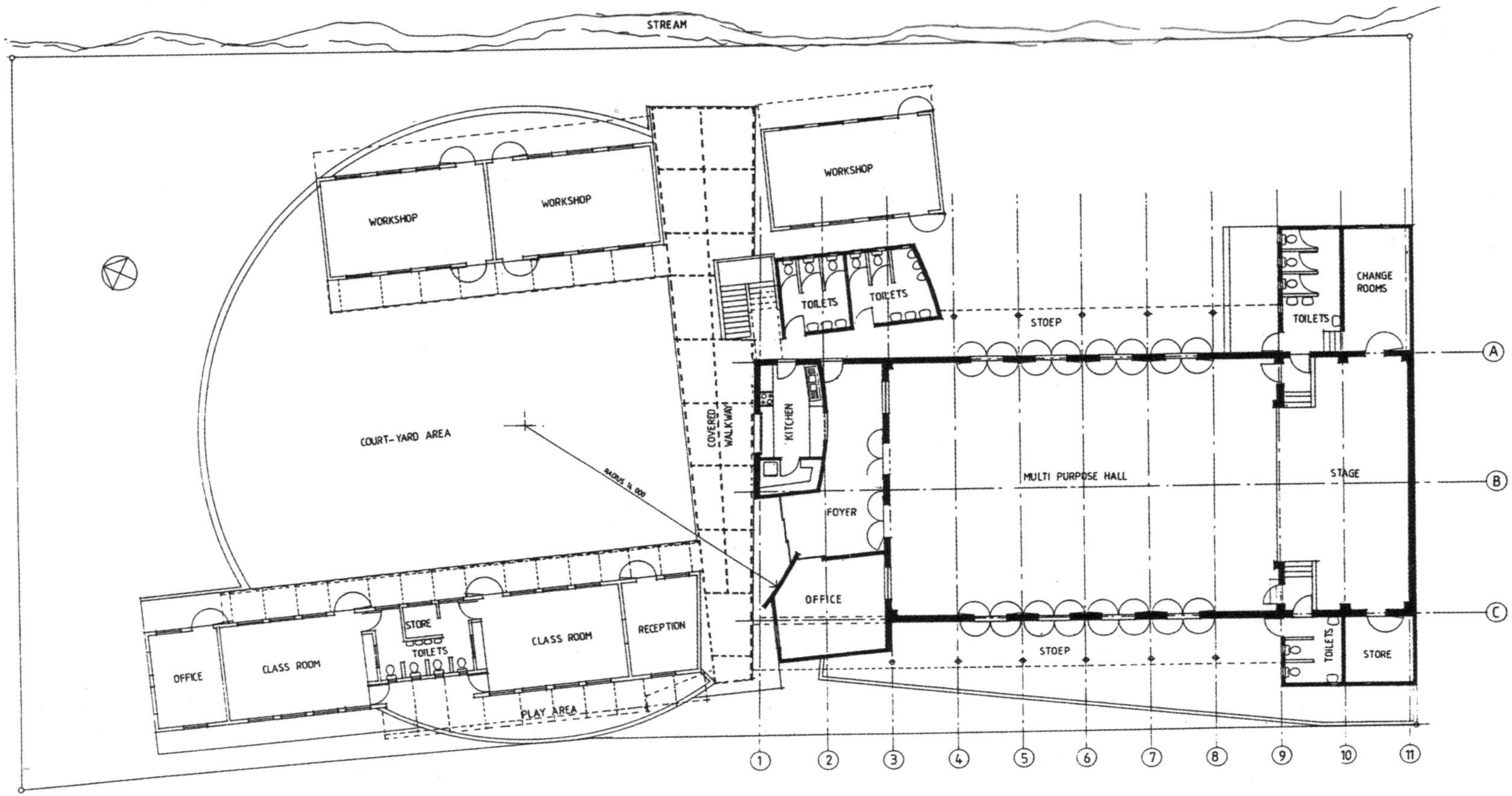
STREAM
WORKSHOP
WORKSHOP
WORKSHOP
TOILETS
TOILETS
STOEP
TOILETS
CHANGE ROOMS
COURT-YARD AREA
COVERED WALKWAY
KITCHEN
RADIUS 14 000
MULTI PURPOSE HALL
STAGE
FOYER
OFFICE
STOEP
STORE
TOILETS
STORE
OFFICE
CLASS ROOM
TOILETS
CLASS ROOM
RECEPTION
PLAY AREA
A
B
C
1
2
3
4
5
6
7
8
9
10
11

ZOLANI MULTIPURPOSE CULTURAL CENTRE,
PHASE I AND II, NYANGA, WESTERN CAPE, 1997-2002,
CS STUDIO ARCHITECTS /////////

Located 15 kilometres from central Cape Town, Nyanga is one of the oldest townships, one of the most exposed to the endemic ills that affect these areas like unemployment, gangsterism and general poor living conditions. At a major crossroads opposite the bus station and a taxi rank, this project is located in an area of relatively central activities: a fruit and vegetable market, clothing shops, areas designated for animal slaughtering, etc. The intersection sees the obligatory daily passage of thousands of commuters. The facility was established in the 1950s and, unlike so many others, pretty well survived and functioned during the years of apartheid. The initial job for CS Studio Architects was to propose a restoration and extension but the allocated budget was too small. The first initiative was the business of a disabled man called Isaac Siyatu who met Carin at the Vukuhambe project, literally meaning "Get up and walk". It consisted of a small structure built in 1986 by CS Studio Architects, created by transforming a simple row of garages.

The project process deeply engaged with users, so much that the project went through a considerable evolution during its design. Imagine the situation when the first meeting to define the specifications saw the gathering of 700 people.

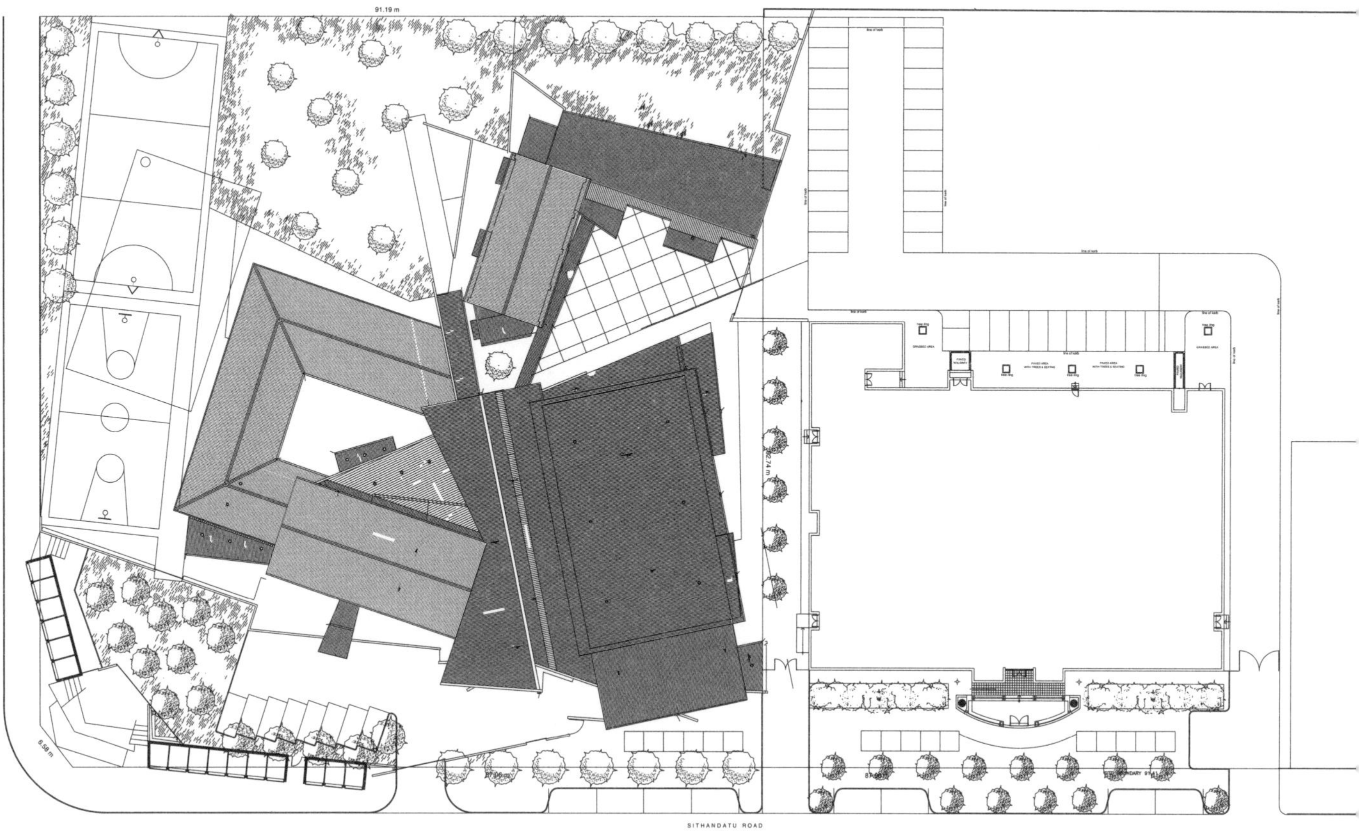

The centre's shape is unlike the orthogonal urban structure, it provides an arrangement of volumes in line with the usual paths, carefully identified and mapped. This system perpetuates the former uses of the site; it also facilitates the integration of the existing buildings in the new project. Even the old facades retain their identity and expressive value. The ensemble is a virtuoso game between the old and the new; sheer reinforced concrete walls support roofs opening to light wells, looking to the sky.

Since 2001 the indoor sports facilities are used intensively, even by world-class athletes. At the same time it is in these rooms that thousands of people receive their monthly pension allowances. Zolani blends behaviours, structures space, and lets the best of contemporary architecture sing.

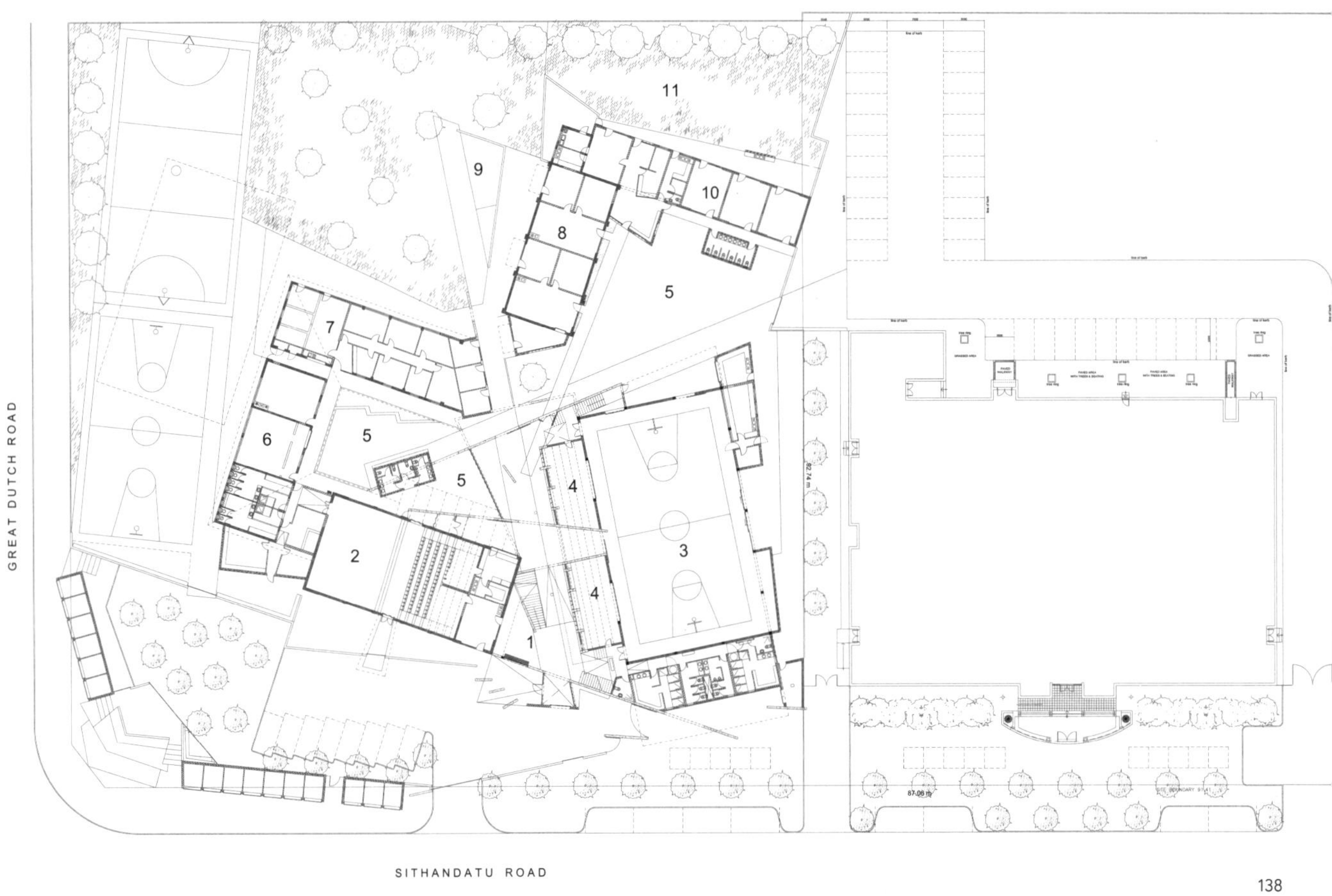

THREE SEA PORTS
/////////

NAVAL BASE
SIMON'S TOWN, WESTERN CAPE, 2007-2020,
EQUITY STUDIO (PTY) LTD
/////////

In recent decades, from Malmö to Barcelona, European port cities have opened up the delights of the waterfront, and with it property speculation. The movement has taken on global proportions and coastlines are gaining attractiveness everywhere. Some projects, such as in China, take the metamorphosis to hand with a focus on the relationship with the natural environment. In Cape Province this trend has taken unique forms. The port of Cape Town has maintained its maritime activity and developed an interesting mix of functions. Like in Barcelona, the visitor now wanders in the once restricted port area, but in Cape Town maritime activity continues. The result is a very stimulating atmosphere, quite different from the exclusively tourist-commercial scenery now dominating the Catalan port.

South of Cape Town, on the Cape peninsula's eastern front facing False Bay, Simon's Town is a pretty town with Victorian houses overlooking the harbour. It is in fact at the centre of strategic facilities of the South African Navy. The first naval facility consisting of a protective dam was built by a Dutch colonial company in 1768. The future Admiral Nelson made port in May 1776, but it was not until May 1814 that the British Royal Navy established its headquarters for the southern Atlantic. The naval base has all the necessary equipment for the fleet's maintenance and provision. It played a key role in the Empire's war efforts during World War II. It was followed by a significant economic boom and a relative integration of the skilled workforce, regardless of their ethnicity. Before 1965 churches, choirs and local life expressed the interdependence of communities, as unequal as they were. This particular fact explains why Simon's Town responded very negatively to the tightening of the rules of segregation in 1965. The council even decided against their application. They were imposed nevertheless, and the absolute rules of apartheid had catastrophic effects on the local economy, which literally collapsed. The naval base, transferred to the South African government in 1957, hosts an exercise facility for evacuation training of German design 209-class submarines. The Republic of South Africa operates three such units engaging in actions against piracy and monitoring fisheries. The development of the training centre required the demolition of an old wooden police station.

This facility for submarine evacuation simulations is unique on the African continent and posed some challenging technical problems regarding the coordination of the various services around the nearly six-floor deep "swimming pool". On the bottom of the pool sits a copy of the central section of a submarine vessel, with a turret containing the evacuation lock. Two men equipped with special suits leave the section and enter the airlock. The airlock is closed, filled with water taken from the ballast so as not to unbalance the vessel, opened to the outside where the men find themselves under 14 metres of water and then have to rise to the surface gradually, step-by-step. The submarine is one of the most critical machines regarding the interface with man; every move can cost lives. The training of submariners (forty-five crew members on a mission, so at least two crews per vessel) covers all functions on board, meaning the mission of every man can be filled by any other; during the Second World War, submarines were lost due to over-specialization in the training of team members. Everything in this simulator is technical, hydraulic, electrical or pneumatic.

There was a considerable risk that the building would only serve to equip the machine with a body. CS Studio Architects has avoided this with great elegance. The pool's steel cylinder is mounted in a wider cylinder consisting of a reinforced concrete structure filled with fair-faced brickwork. Its base houses the machinery, on top of which locker rooms as well as service rooms are arranged concentrically. Executive offices are upstairs, accessible by a walkway. Vertical circulation is found in two separate towers, one of concrete for the elevator, the other of steel for the stairs. As there is no denying that the functions determine the forms of this building, they do so in a fine dialectical way, leaving sufficient room for formulating an architecture that is expressive, formally stable by itself, and consistent. As a counterpoint, some anecdotal information has put me on the track of this argument: I have never heard of Carin Smuts and Urs Schmid explaining that the customer's requirements, contingencies of the construction site, or the accuracy of the budget would have

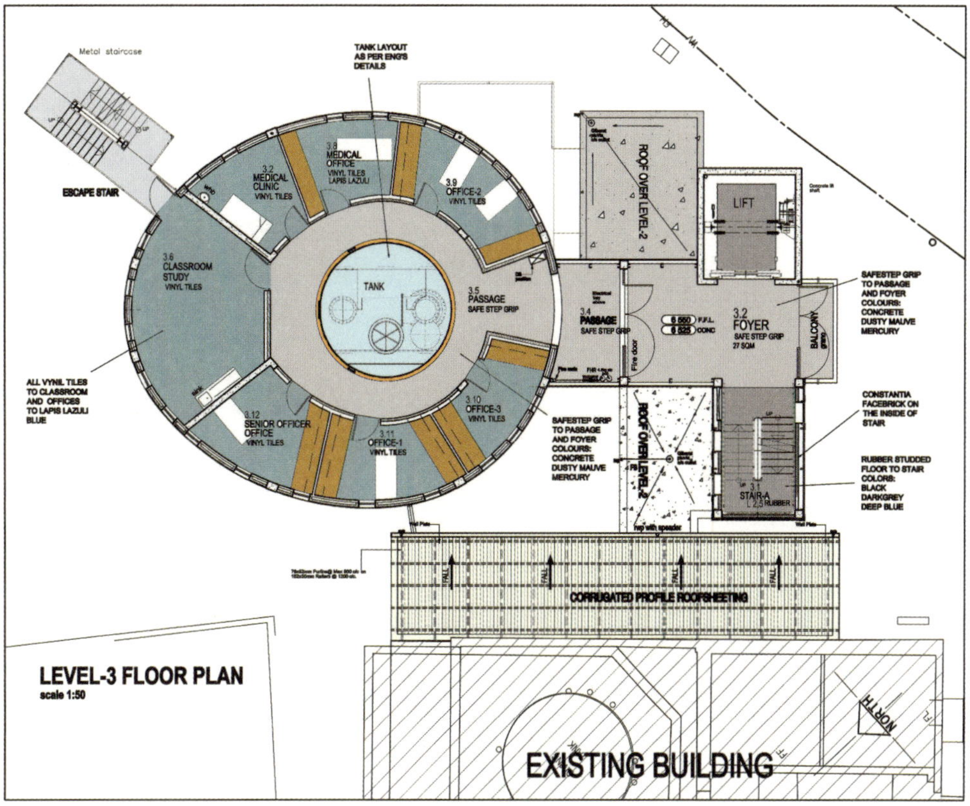

"forced" them, or would have "not let them the choice". Such an explanation is typical of those who, devoid of talent, sideline themselves through admitting by speaking of it. This project reminds me of Ettore Bugatti, known for carving his engine blocks in wood prior to arranging his incredible mechanisms whose technical characteristics, innovations, and thus forms, were present in his mind when visualizing the ensemble.

An important part of the activities of an independent architectural office in South Africa is oriented towards the public sector, access to which is subject to the acceptance of a binding programme of requirements regarding quota and equal opportunities. The order for a submarine simulator for the Navy of the Republic of South Africa requires a considerable effort regarding adaptation to these conditions. In this type of commission, CS Studio Architects applies a similar approach as in community projects. The same attention is paid to user needs, their culture, and ways to meet the programmatic requirements. It is known that submariners have an extremely precise and demanding etiquette, which allows them to deal with the extreme overcrowding conditions on board. The personal space of the individual is reduced to a minimum and physical contact, even accidental, is strictly forbidden. This special world poses a conundrum to the architect. First, they must deliver a building constructed according to the rules of use and stability, striving to provide spaces, shapes, materials and colours so as to provide satisfactory comfort, while simultaneously simulating the cruellest and most uncomfortable relations ever of this man-machine and human-environment. Seen from the exterior,[1] the result does not appear out of place in the small Victorian town of Simon's Town; one wonders if the architects in charge of such a programme did not already have its recycling for more creative purposes in mind.

1 Like other such plants, the base is not publicly accessible; the documents published are those on the agency's website.

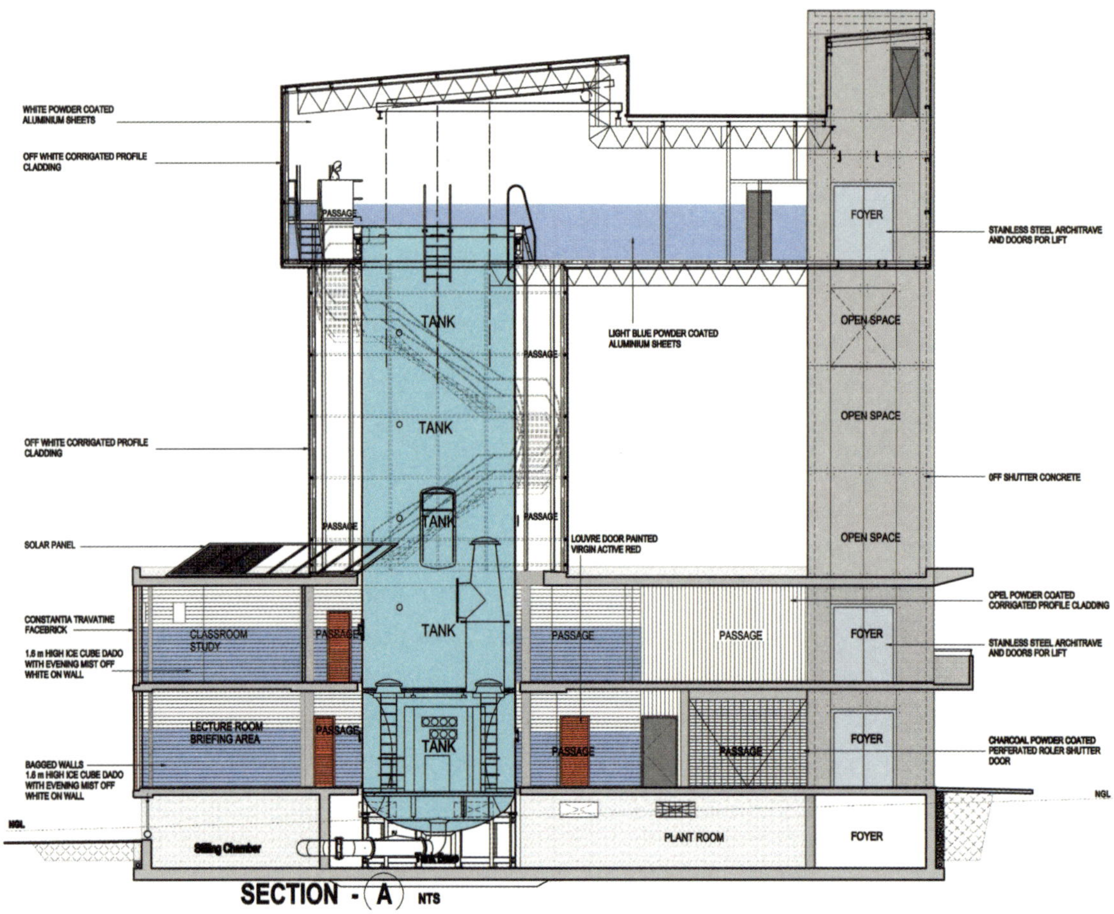

SOUTH AFRICAN MILITARY
HEALTH SERVICE
BKX 977M

THREE SEA PORTS
/////////

REDEVELOPMENT OF PORT FACILITIES GANSBAAI, WESTERN CAPE, 2007-2010, CS STUDIO ARCHITECTS
/////////

EDEL WEISS
DDF 267 P

From Simon's Town to Gansbaai, you either navigate heading south-east towards Hermanus Bay or take the northern and then the coastal route to Eastern Cape. Gansbaai is a fishing port whose facilities required upgrading and redevelopment.

Interventions are discreet and effective. They draw from the catalogue of countless tricks that CS Studio Architects developed over the years. The solutions are constructive, spatial and chromatic. It is in vain that the architecture lover would seek the costly subtleties that criticism calls "attention to detail". Therefore details are not neglected, and the use of an economical standard solution, like basic door and window ironmongery or sanitary ware, is systematically governed by scale, colour and the relationship between elements.

There, where circumstances would have established a sentry box of miserable pragmatism showing an inhospitable facade, a few courses of bricks and a properly placed awning create a link with the other elements, beginning a dialogue, and giving expression to a function. The affair of architecture draws strength from consideration for users. Not only of colour and of polychrome material; the ceramic tiles are hygienic and vandal proof, they mark a spatial unity, a continuum that can be spectacular or, on the contrary, appear subtly.

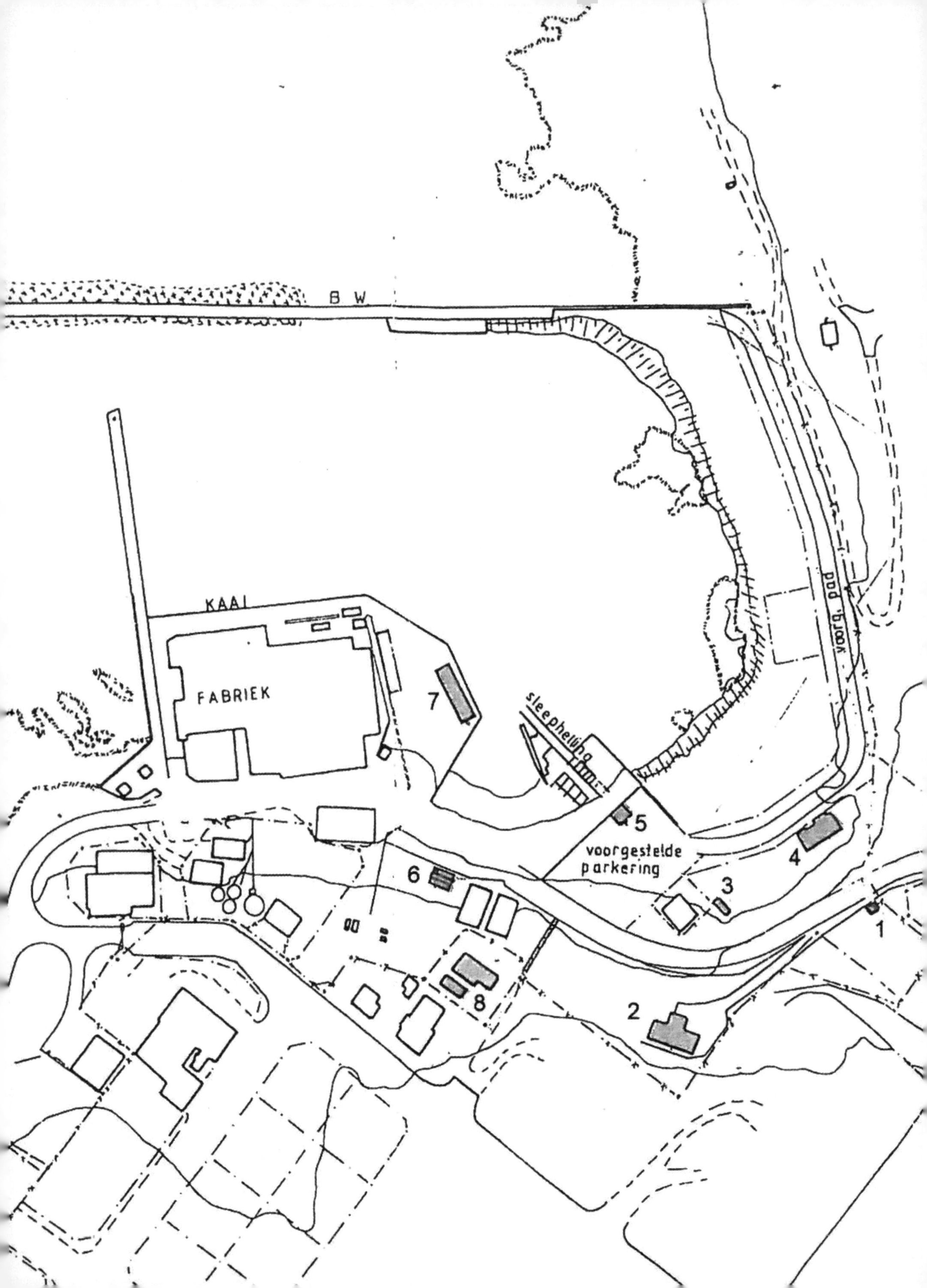
B W
KAAI
FABRIEK
7
sleephelling
voorg. pad
5
voorgestelde parkering
6
4
3
1
8
2

THREE SEA PORTS
/////////

LUJIAZHI CULTURAL CREATIVITY GARDEN
ZHOUSHAN, CHINA
2010-2015, CS STUDIO ARCHITECTS
/////////

The two preceding projects were the perfect preparation for meeting the specifications of this project. Led by Amateur Architecture Studio (Wang Shu and Lu Wenyu), commissioned by the local government, and in collaboration with the French Institute of Architecture (Marie-Hélène Contal) and the LOCUS Foundation (Professor Jana Revedin), this project has mobilized fourteen architects who have received the Global Award for Sustainable Architecture (2007 to 2009), to participate in a project on the occasion of the Shanghai World Expo. Meanwhile, the LOCUS Foundation was asked to develop a practical project on the site.

Organized in a workshop that brought all the participants together in a start-up process, a draw at the very beginning attributed them each two lots to be redeveloped in the dense area. CS Studio Architects received shared lots 6a–6b and 13, and proposed building a maritime museum, artists' workshops and residential studios. An ice factory, a remnant of the industrial services typical of this fishing port, was asked to stay. The various buildings on the site are connected by a canopy, reminiscent of the conveyor belts that are so typical of industrial facilities. According to the latest information (September 2015), the entire site was sold to a property developer and a corrosive uncertainty now shrouds this set of projects launched in 2010. The observer cannot help to see a connection with the cases of Hawston, Follainville-Dennemont and even the Helsinki competition to emphasize that if architecture in thirty years has become a powerful vector in the affirmation of urban identities, it is too often held hostage by politicians and developers who are keen to take advantage of a momentum arisen in the wake of a creative endeavour and to one way or another confiscate the fallout.

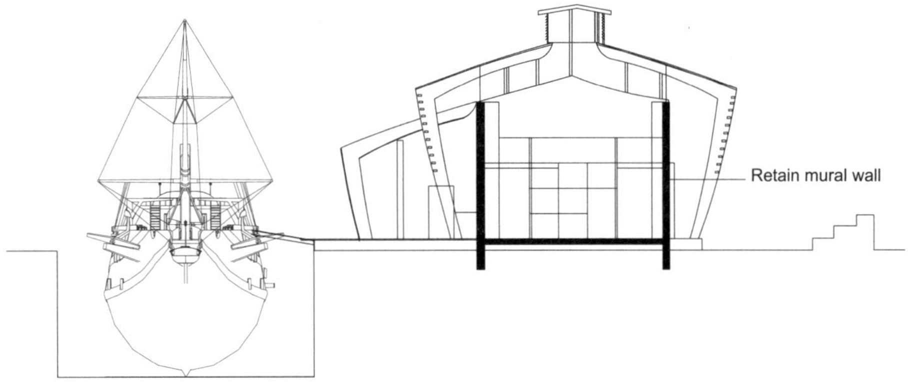

SECTION A-A

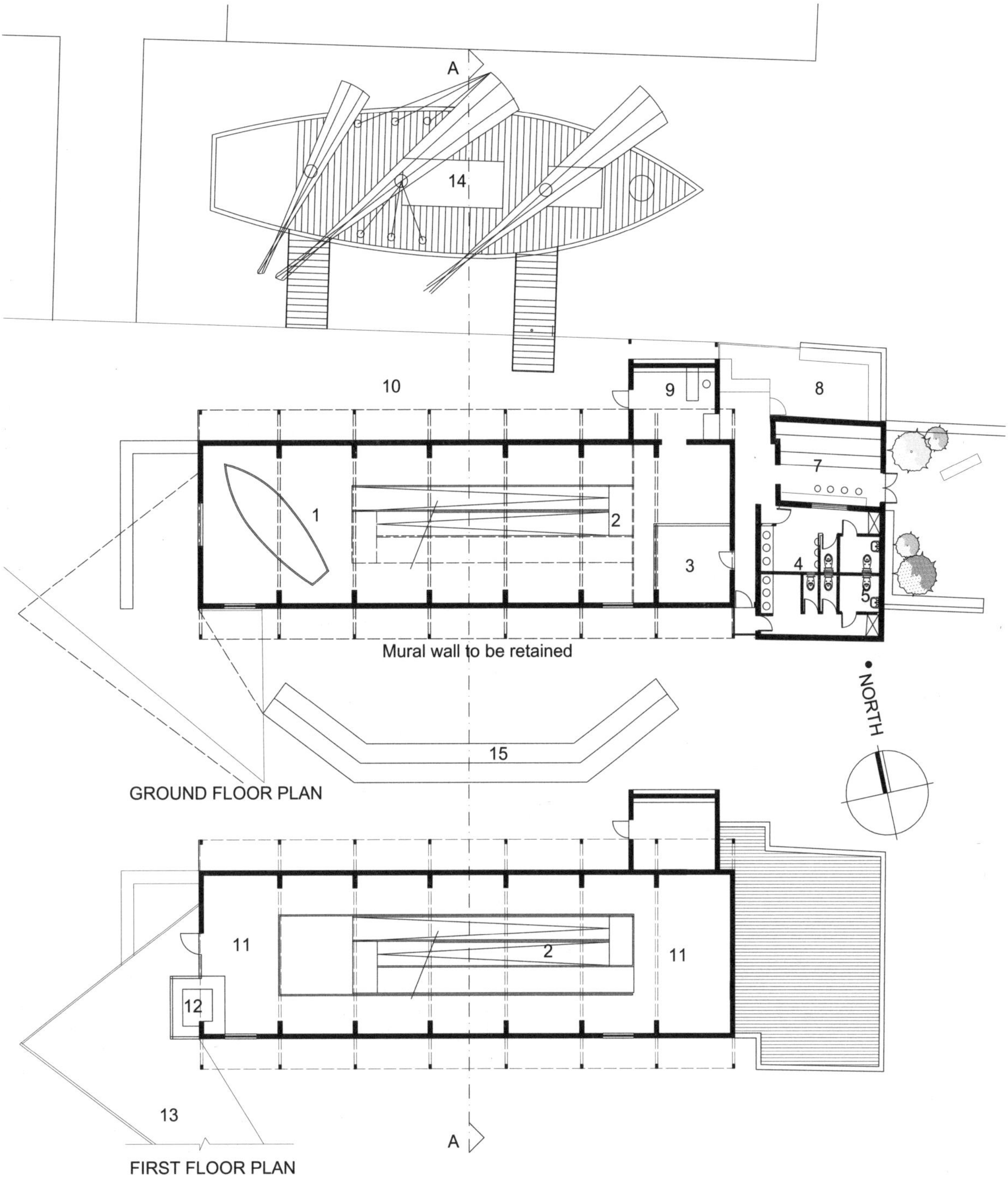

A
14
10
9
8
7
1
2
3
4
5
Mural wall to be retained
NORTH
15
GROUND FLOOR PLAN
11
2
11
12
13
A
FIRST FLOOR PLAN

HELDERSTROOM PRISON, CANTEEN, SPORTS AND RECREATIONAL FACILITIES FOR STAFF, STORE & PETROL STATION, HELDERSTROOM CALEDON, WESTERN CAPE, 2001-2009, CS STUDIO ARCHITECTS

This project was commissioned and built on behalf of the National Department of Public Works, with CS Studio Architects in charge of the overall planning, landscape design and construction of the facilities mentioned in the title. CS Studio Architects worked in association with Sudhier Magan Architects whose mandate covered the standardized family houses.

This high-security prison is located in the rural district of Caledon, 110 kilometres south-east of Cape Town, and sits atop a hill with steep slopes on the territory of the farm that gave it its name. Initially the farm buildings were used to house various services; housing needs were satisfied with temporary facilities.

The master plan proposed by CS Studio Architects makes use of the existing spontaneous arrangement of caravans and locates facilities east of the prison proper. It skilfully groups functions, areas and activities, and sorts traffic. CS Studio Architects' draft called the standard plans of the prison administration into question; initially, under the leadership of Mr Damstra, this amendment was approved. His successor, Mr Crafford, although having arrived relatively late on the project, challenged it. In particular he imposed a north-south orientation of the buildings, placing them perpendicular to the contour lines, or perpendicular to the approved project.

CS Studio Architects responded by placing service buildings in the area with the gentlest slope, still out of reach of potential flooding by the nearby stream, and by putting housing for single workers on the slope. In both cases, circulation is afforded by ramps cleverly getting around the constraint of the mandatory orientation. The sections show this perfectly. The service building's entanglement of the masses, volumes and circulation defy description. After walking it, a seemingly contradictory given leaves a deep impression in one's memory: the parts and functions are in close proximity and keep a safe distance at the same time. One perceives in the spaces, afforded by the delicate use of materials, as always governed conducting of light and the careful attention paid early in the project to the experience as well as the needs of users. This kind of "participation'" is not just a checkbox in a bureaucratic process; rather, it creates space and time for the creative force of a collective to develop. Where the standards imposed by the project's developer would say "impossible" to many architects, or serve as a pretext for reprehensible pragmatism, CS Studio Architects manages to ultimately make a virtue of necessity. For individual housing the standard attributes a generous 11 square metres to a prison service officer. It should be noted that in practice this amounts to accommodating three to five people in this space. These people have indeed children and should, because of their jobs in the prison service, be accompanied by an aid or a nanny to look after them. The standard ascribes 17 square metres of leisure space to fourteen rooms. Placing these areas with the best exposure to the sun (north in the southern hemisphere), facing the open landscape and in front of the neighbouring unit's laundry

room , affords an environment that is full of social interaction and thus can overcome its nominal smallness. The architectural expression, the colours and the materials borrow from the repertoire of local rural architecture.

The very few meetings held with prison centre staff revealed that their feelings are accurately expressed by the request: “Please, make us a village.” Therefore in this project the master plan and the landscape aspect of architecture are particularly important. CS Studio Architects considers them an essential part of its mission, a fundamental task of the architect. The plantations are made of local species requiring little maintenance and no watering. The num-num (Carissa macrocarpa) for example planted in front of windows, is both a safety feature because of its branches with sharp thorns and a source of fruits rich in vitamin C. Helderstroom is located at the cross roads of the Cape province wine routes, evidenced by the many stopping-off points for wine tourists, the “gardens” entirely fabricated by fashionable landscape architects. These are all specimens of exotic kitsch, but criticism of flowerbeds is a different affair.

CRADOCK VISION 2000, URBAN DEVELOPMENT PLAN
CRADOCK, EASTERN CAPE, 1994-1995, CS STUDIO ARCHITECTS
/////////

"... enough men had gone off to war
saying the time of gardening was
when the war was over;
whereas there must be men to stay behind
and keep gardening alive, or at least the idea of gardening;
because once that cord was broken,
the earth would grow hard and forget her children.
That was why."

— J. M. Coetzee, *Michael K., His Life, His Time.*

The first projects by CS Studio Architects in the historic bastion of the struggle against apartheid in the Eastern Cape consisted of a crèche and a library; later came a dispensary. The circumstances of the establishment of these facilities highlight the violent effects of apartheid on the opportunity to own land and the freedom to settle. The consequences of this policy of severing people from their land, of ordering their arbitrary displacement, would be felt deeply and at length after the unjust regime had formally disappeared. Even today an impressive amount of housing built by the South African government offices is being built on orthogonal grids, characteristic of yesterday's townships. The Cradock Vision 2000 project had the ambition to accomplish a subdivision plan and realize buildings with deep involvement of future residents. The available resources were very modest and the plots allocated to each household were small (240 square metres). It was necessary to establish an infrastructure and promote self-help. For efficiency, a general contractor was responsible for the infrastructure work we would call "utilities" or "services". A jackpot system called *gooi-gooi* successively enabled slum households to finance basic construction. To avoid the excesses often observed in operations that make people very poor owners of a plot, strict rules oblige beneficiaries to be the exclusive users in order to avoid leasing, debts and the eventuation of grabbing mechanisms. Intuitive experience teaches that the free market works well as long as it is closely supervised. Simultaneously with this operation, 150 "family gardens" were established in a fertile bend of the river below.

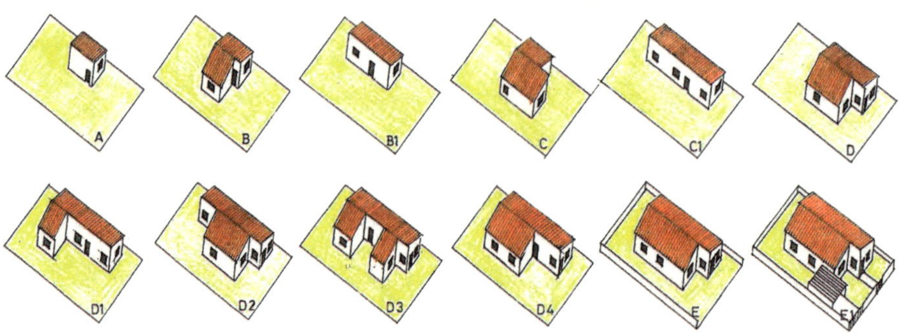

RIVERSDALE MAGISTRATES COURT, RESTORATION AND ENLARGEMENT, RIVERSDALE, WESTERN CAPE, 2007-2011, CS STUDIO ARCHITECTS /////////

The original building was restored in a both conserving and "sustainable" way, based on the idea that the intervention should aim at maintaining the building's civic image on the street, improving its functional performance and restoring its architectural features. At the same time, the architects were asked to integrate and articulate an extension that would triple its useful surfaces.

The highly symbolic neoclassical and neo-colonial identity had to be preserved and neutralized. The architects achieved this surprisingly, by concentrating on a new requirement, that of an access ramp for wheelchair users. Instead of considering it a burden and an obstacle, they skilfully took it as leverage for creating a new main entrance on the side, which opens through an air lock to a corridor and a courtyard. These latter connect on the right to the old building whose Palladian entrance, crystallized in its renovation, will be dedicated to services and thus become symbolically obsolete. On their left they lead to the important contemporary addition. Shaded courtyards provide a comfortable climate, enabling the enjoyment of the daylight, and structuring circulation. In its expanded form, the Riversdale Court of Justice occupies the entire island. In structuring access to buildings, CS Studio Architects often explores the possibilities of the ramp, taking advantage of a technical constraint to build a spatial organization around the means to overcome it. This is particularly visible in the access to the recently completed Delft Symphony Way clinic.[1]

3
See page 84.

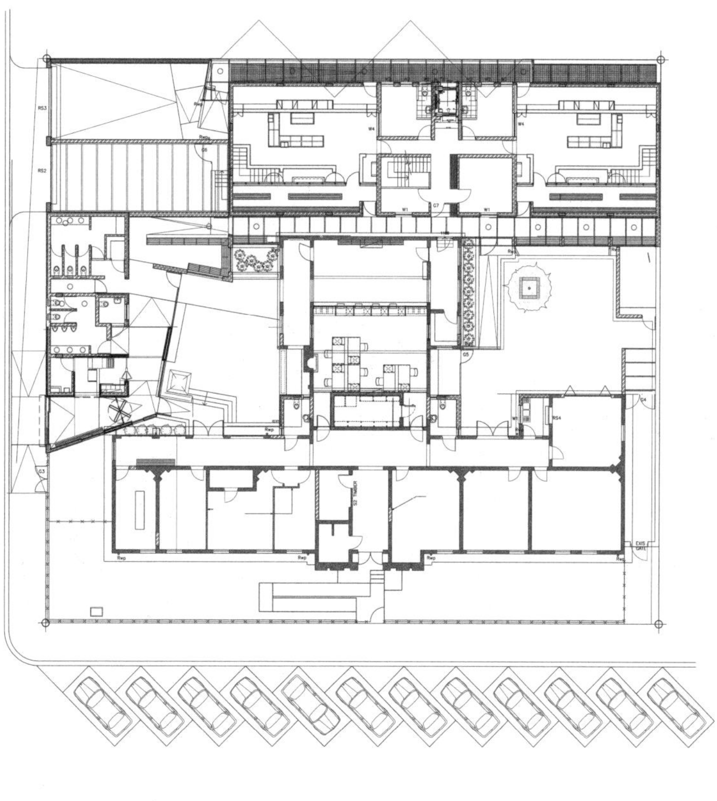

GROUND PLAN LAYOUT

HAWSTON TOURISM GATEWAY
HAWSTON, HERMANUS, WESTERN CAPE, PLANNED IN 2015,
CS STUDIO ARCHITECTS /////////

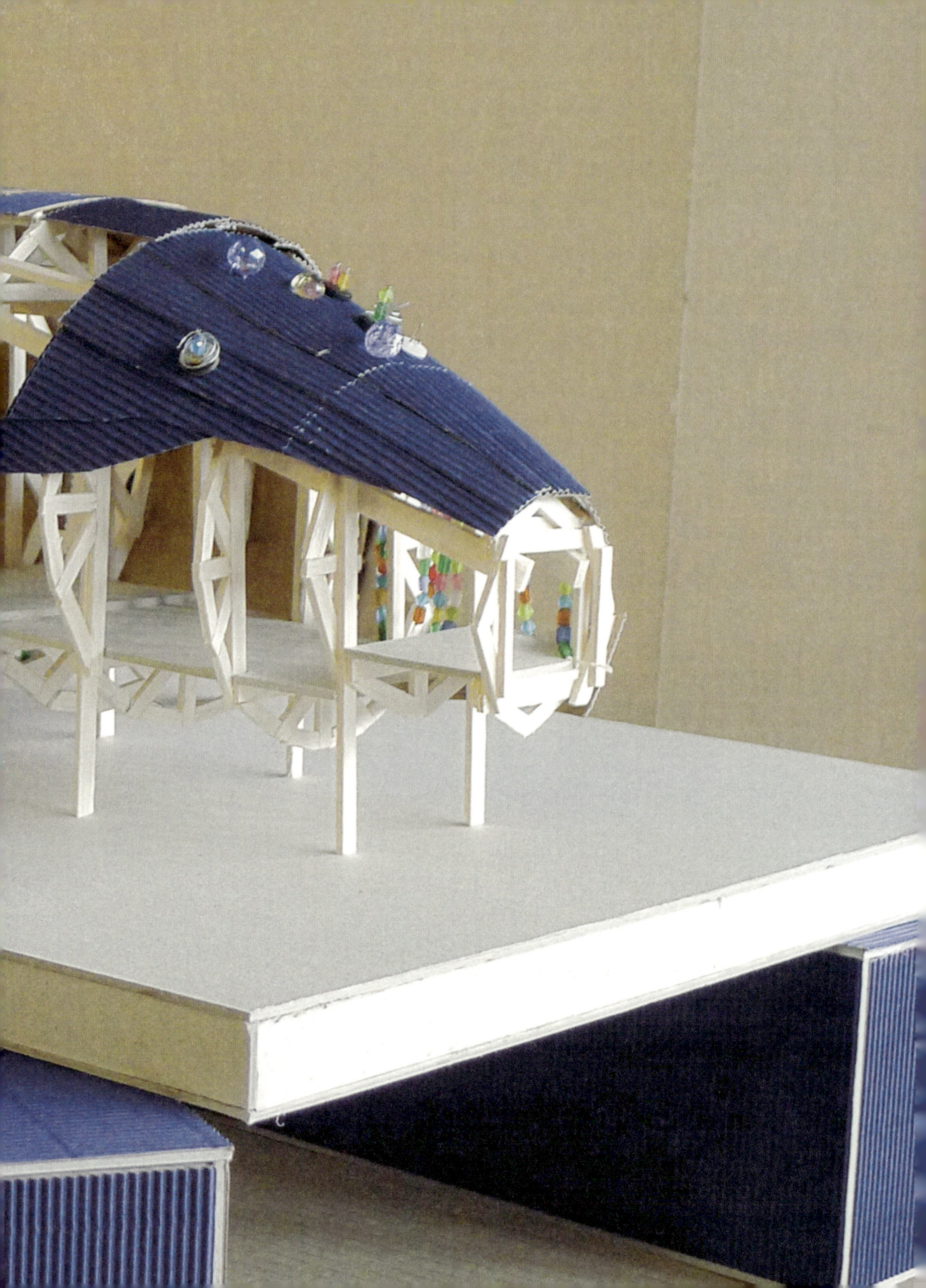

Paradoxically and despite its extravagances that have degenerated to mere mannerism, the international architecture scene is, in short, of a staggering uniformity. Everything has been done, everything has been imitated hundreds of times, and hundreds of times been degraded. Judging by the copies, the models are reduced to clichés. Like the Bilbao Guggenheim, which could be credited with originality provided one ignores the miserable ratio of usable to constructed surface, hundreds of by-products "mime [it] limping".[1] The procedures of international competitions are controlled by leading architects and reviewed by cohorts of punctilious officials and picky lawyers, so much so that, barring a few rare exceptions, it selects only the avatars of clichés, the so called "opinion leaders". Real creativity is structurally kept out. This phenomenon is seen at all levels of competition procedures, international as well as local. Everywhere, the design competition has become a useful cog in the awarding of public contracts; it has drifted far away from the "experimental tradition".[2]

This dark preamble helps one appreciate at full value the inventive tricks that CS Studio Architects implements in order to unleash the idea of its project. By organizing an open for all ideas competition called "visioning drawings" together with the inhabitants of Hawston, who were fed up with the pressure of gangs and abalone poachers, the architects created conditions that helped absolutely free and unconventional ideas to emerge. The models give an idea of how these are at the origin of the joyful project.

1
Charles Baudelaire, *L'Albatros* (1859).

2
Barry Bergdoll, *The Experimental Tradition: Essays on Competitions in Architecture*, New York: Princeton Architectural Press, 1989.

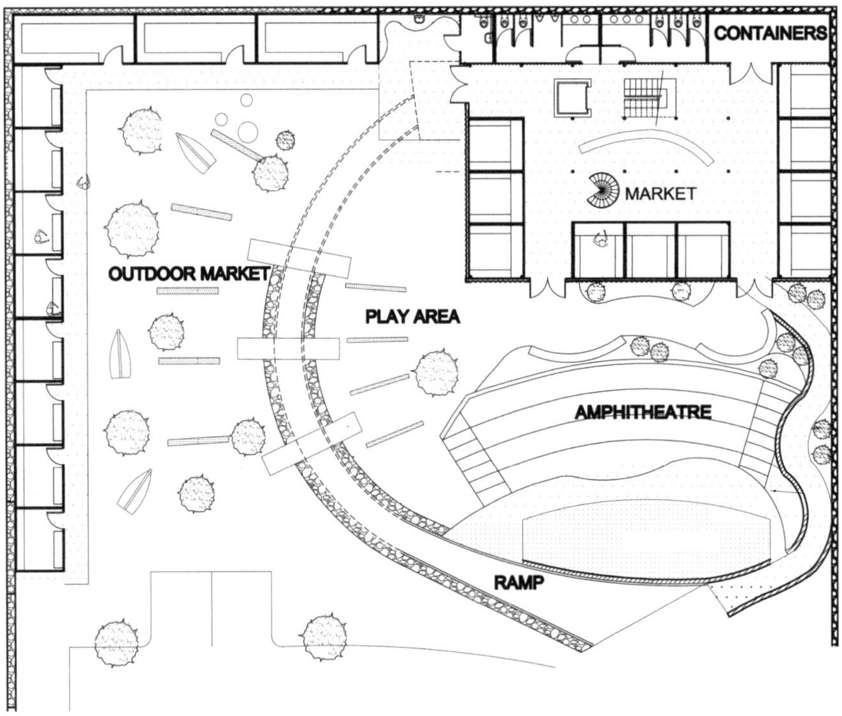

The programme consists of installing an aquarium around which various commercial activities can aggregate and thus stimulate the local economy. The ramp, its semi-circular shape defining a perfect outdoor amphitheatre, gives access to the upper levels while an elevator ride serves the whale floating 30 metres above the ground. The belly of the whale allows visitors to enjoy the information provided by a marine life theme centre; through its ears they can see whales frolic in the bay and perhaps ponder the notion of perspective in architecture.

The idea is to recycle shipping containers for the shell of this cultural project. It is understood as a cornerstone of local economic development capable of creating jobs and training opportunities. Very early, the spectacular model turned out to be the dreamlike catalyst for the project. It makes the dream of being Jonah that slumbers in all of us immediately comprehensible. Carin Smuts drew from literature, especially novels of deserted islands[3] to feed her thoughts about the needs of isolated populations, left to themselves as if shipwrecked.

In early 2016 there was bad news; against a background of corruption, local authorities are hindering the project's development. This again draws attention to the civic responsibility of the architect; to be like a lifeless fish going with the flow or to be a member of the resistance acting according to their conscience.

3 J. M. Coetzee, *Foe*, London: Penguin Books, 1988.

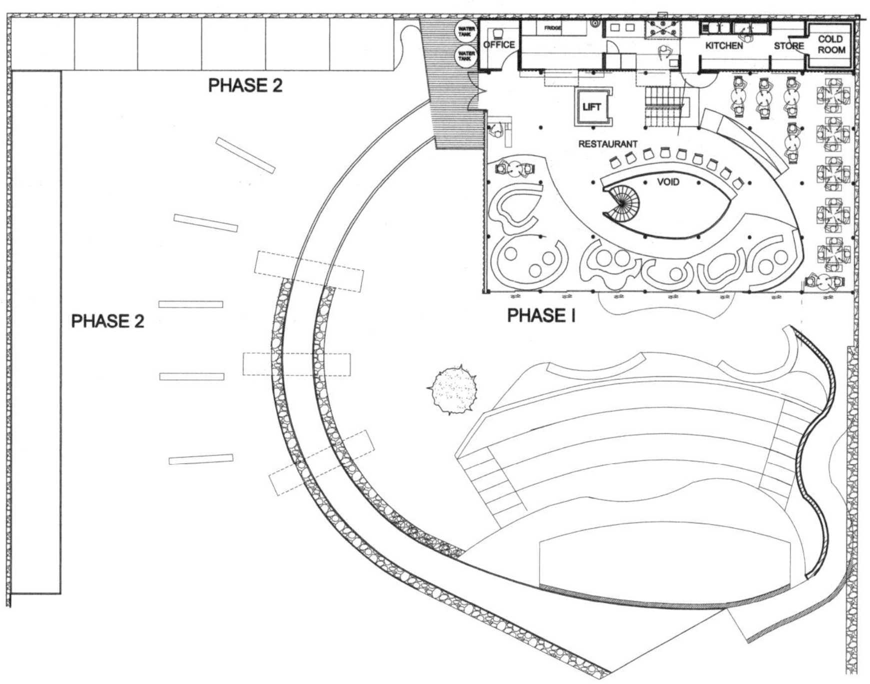

GROOTVADERSBOSCH NATURE RESERVE, RENOVATION OF RECEPTION AND ACCOMMODATION FACILITIES HEIDELBERG, WESTERN CAPE, CAPE NATURE, 2012-2016, EQUITY STUDIO (PTY) LT

The renovation of the infrastructure of this natural reserve in Cape Province was designed to afford strict economy of materials, optimization of recycling, and precise assessment of the environmental impact. The area was divided into two zones. The first includes the administrative building, the reception areas, and three houses for staff. The second comprises 32 logger huts, of which 21 were disassembled, the materials sorted and stored for use in the reconstruction. The others were subject to a renovation programme that aims at opening them to nature, equipping them with modern sanitation, changing the number of rooms from four to two, thus allowing the creation of a living room. By adding a veranda functioning as terrace and transitional space, the architect created a space open to nature. Initially, this part was thought of as a covered gallery, but that vision had to give way to a more realistic choice since at night, baboons come out of the forest and take control of the space. The coexistence however, is difficult. Building materials were reused as much as possible in this project. Despite the low cost of labour, the contractor to whom the work was awarded considered the process "expensive". He pointed at the amount of preservation work, restoration of removed items, and the many changes in the project made necessary by adaptation to the available materials. Besides that, the origin of the materials also articulates the differences between the houses.

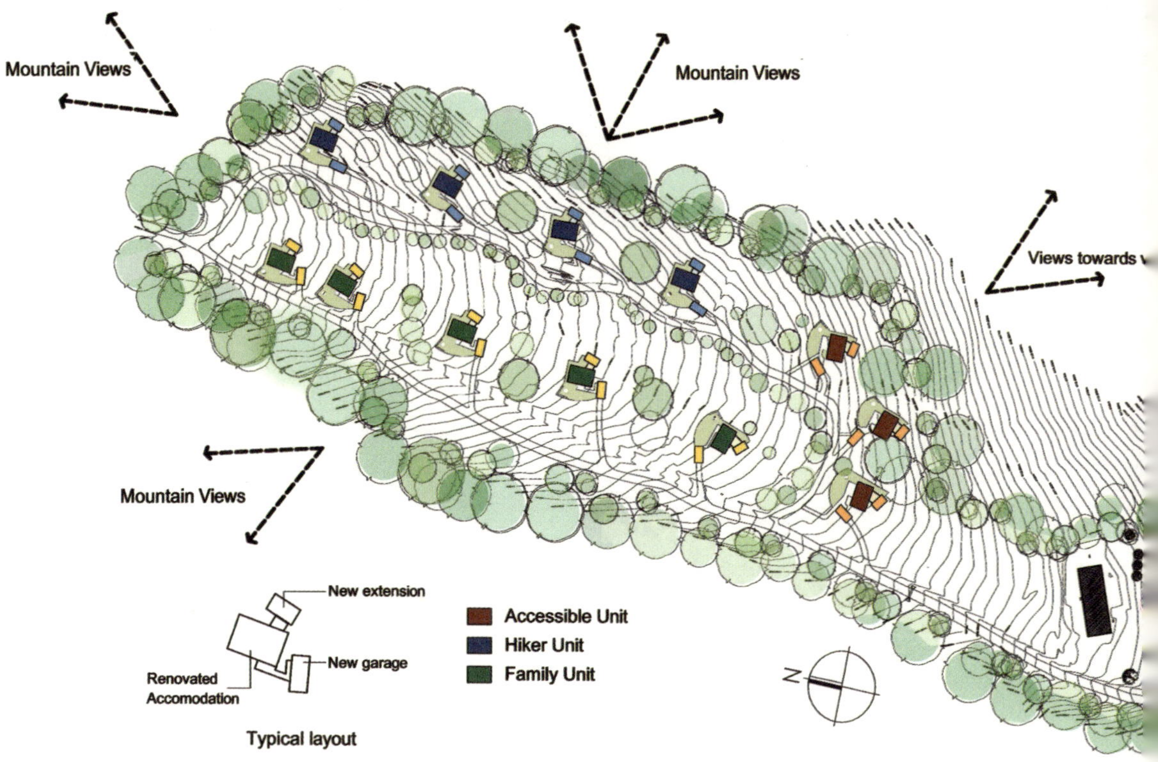

GUGULETHU CENTRAL MEAT MARKET
WESTERN CAPE, 1996-1998, CS STUDIO ARCHITECTS
/////////

Simba
Cash Store
VIVA
Cash Store
3
CA 505-636

How to organize active traders on the retail market and at the same time build a structure where customers and merchants can meet? This problem occurred in South Africa after the end of apartheid gave rise to the redeployment, at least geographically, of urban services.

The problem is similar to those of nineteenth-century Europe; it is interesting to see how it was addressed by the School of Fine Arts in Paris. In his *Éléments et théorie de l'architecture*, Julien Guadet explains the ancient traditions of the forum and the bazaar, and comes to the conclusion that they are inadequate. One may feel some reluctance towards Guadet as a person not very keen on opportunities to make great architecture, but he insightfully points out major problems boiling down to three elements: broad coverage, efficient ventilation and how to avoid draughts. Guadet observed how models were unimaginatively copied, followed by copying of copies, and regretted that "the program fell to export-architecture".

Shelter, ventilation, fences and protection from prevailing winds are exactly the functions that the central meat market of Gugulethu perfectly fulfils. An L-shaped building delimits the space, hosts services (sanitary, offices, etc.) and protects against the winds from the south and west. The vast wave-shaped roof plants an iconic landmark in the landscape and thus directs the surrounding traffic. Under this roof, ventilation is very effective yet free from draughts, and thus allows traditional barbecuing. Whereas all this relates to technique and architecture, the market, whose setup was decided in 1994, is the result of a long process that eventually enabled developments going far beyond the definition of a programme, a project, and its construction.

1
Julien Guadet, *Éléments et théorie de l'architecture*, t. II, Paris: Librairie de la construction moderne, 1894.

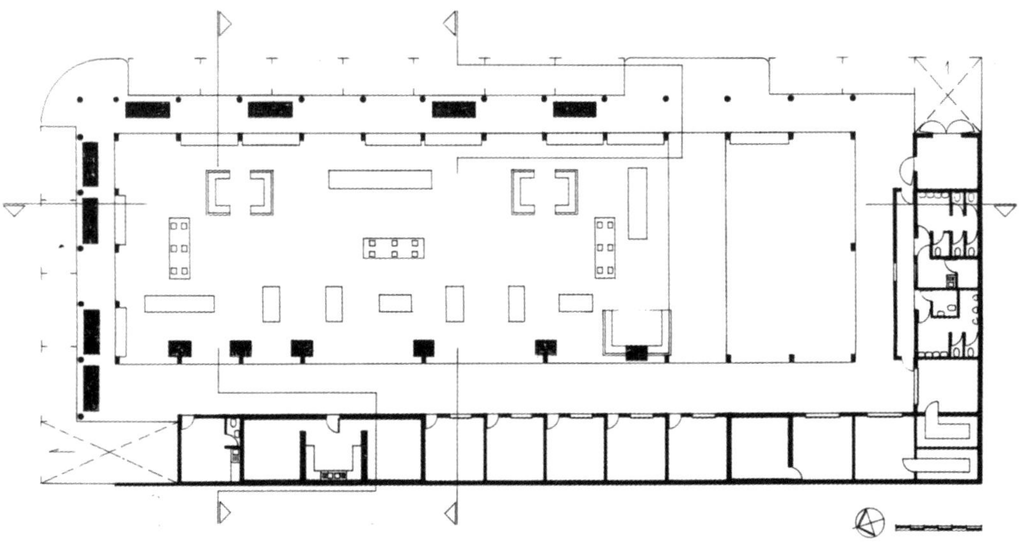

During this project, businesses organized themselves, skills were developed, and ultimately, the social and technical rules of a first and foremost informal sector were applied. British and Canadian institutions as well as a major international trust company brought in skills and disseminated them through workshops, so much so that the market was not only built, but was established. Due to this process Gugulethu has become a kind of civil basilica of this urban area. To take a meal there in company of the architects is a unique experience; one senses the depth of the ties with the merchants, especially the women. Finally, that rapport of the architects with their client after the work has been delivered, is a key and symptomatic indication.

This municipal project funded by the Yvelines General Council, patron of the Global Award for Sustainable Architecture, was to be the second in a series. It aimed at realizing a project in the department designed by an award winner. It did not succeed and the failure is somehow instructive. It highlights, in a way that one could for once call South-North, the cultural, anthropological and administrative issues related to the transfer of know-how.

True to its method, CS Studio Architects set up project workshops to which the inhabitants of two hamlets were invited, for once united. First the children, then the adults. The programme was formulated literally in the mood of "What is your dream?" It highlighted and allowed the expression of specific needs and thus led to the definition of a joint unorthodox program including education, culture, as well as social services. In the image of this unique programme, the form expressed the idea of connecting different areas, of a uniting shelter for multiple functions and resistance to the orthogonality to which in France the republic's institutions have a tendency, similar to the spirits of the public service staff. The activities of the project and its workshops necessitated five trips to France and a host of exchanges, implications and considerable emotion. On the spot, the project had to deal with the usual procedures for updating the land use plan and the urban zoning plan. It created a situation of administrative uncertainty in which the project eventually stalled. Parallel to that reality, whatever the subsidy policies and their vagaries make of it, the mayor has the discretion to issue a building permit, even if contrary to a regulation or the service in charge of issuing. He did not do so; he regained control and thus ensured his authority. According Carin Smuts, the mayor made this clear by saying he wanted a box with two doors that he could close.

RESTRUCTURING OF THE CITY CENTRE, MULTIPURPOSE BUILDING, FOLLAINVILLE-DENNEMONT, YVELINES, FRANCE, 2009, CS STUDIO ARCHITECTS ////////

The lesson learned from this failure is the structural difference between French and South African local governments.[1] In France local governments traditionally provide public buildings to all classes and in all categories. Authorities are deemed to fulfil this mission. There is no room for participation, or at best reduced to a consultation on cosmetic items. In South Africa, CS Studio Architects has a very different position organizing and building infrastructure like the stand-alone projects for the masses with which the agency is closely linked; it substitutes the obstruction or the anarchy of the state.

1 I am grateful to Marie-Hélène Contal for her valuable insights and political acumen. I drew much inspiration from her analysis.

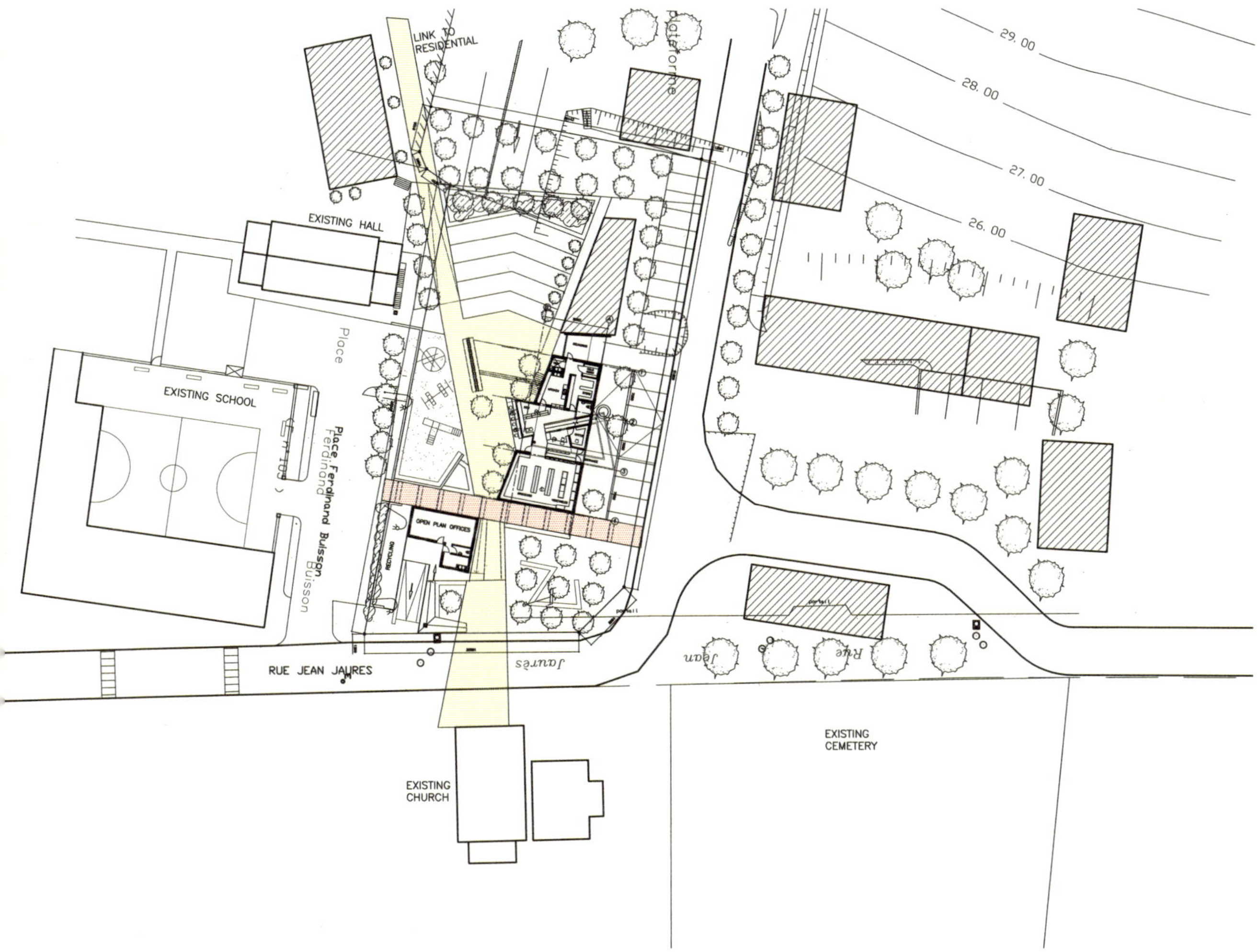

PROJECT RESULTING FROM A COLLABORATION BETWEEN THE YVELINES DEPARTMENT AND THE GLOBAL AWARD FOR SUSTAINABLE ARCHITECTURE

/////////

BLIKKIESDORP, HOUSE AND STUDIO OF THE ARCHITECT, SEAPOINT, CAPE TOWN, WESTERN CAPE, 2005, CS STUDIO ARCHITECTS /////////

To evoke the architect's own house inevitably leads to the well-explored idea of a built self-portrait. The studio house on Cape Town's Ocean View obviously relates to it, but also distinguishes itself by the fact that it is at the same time reinvestment, residence and workplace. It is also an expressive manifesto of the most emblematic projects of CS Studio Architects, to the point of having let crystallize the rejection by neighbours who saw its construction as an extension of the slums into a white residential area. In fact the approach is of a so to speak vernacular character, to the extent that the first bungalows established on the Atlantic coast outside the city were built of corrugated sheets. This argument of filiation from tradition proved decisive at the time of granting the building permit.

NORTH EAST ELEVATION

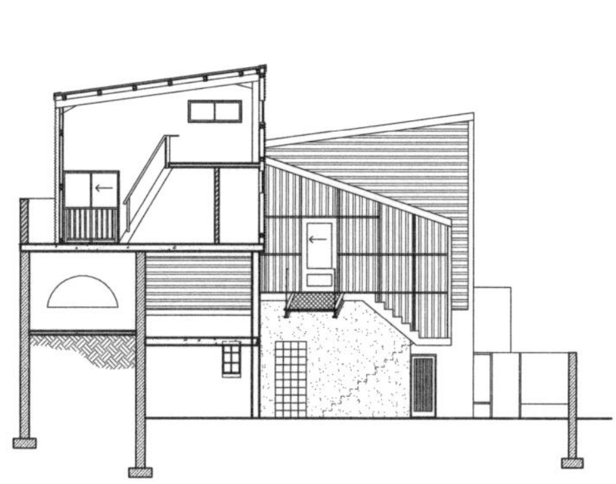

SECTION

Corrugated sheet gives a highly contrasting effect with the houses in this neighbourhood. It is a material common to spatially ruptured areas. By their simple and open volumes, kept to modest dimensions because of objections raised by the neighbours, the elevations confirm the formal break suggested by the materials. The residential area is infested with industrial form, productive function and materials that emphasize difference. Even the colours emphasize the alien character: a green "Umhlanga wave" reflecting the ubiquitous ocean.

The ensemble is designed as an experimental site under permanent construction. A solar energy system will soon be added, giving the site a place in the field of energy production. Carin Smuts deploys her talents as ceramist where ordinary mortals would place tiles. A scale model by sculptor Willie Bester, delivered under the guise of commissioning his house, occupies the terrace. The forms are simple, finishes are rudimentary, art is everywhere; material, creativity and invention are implemented yet in progress.

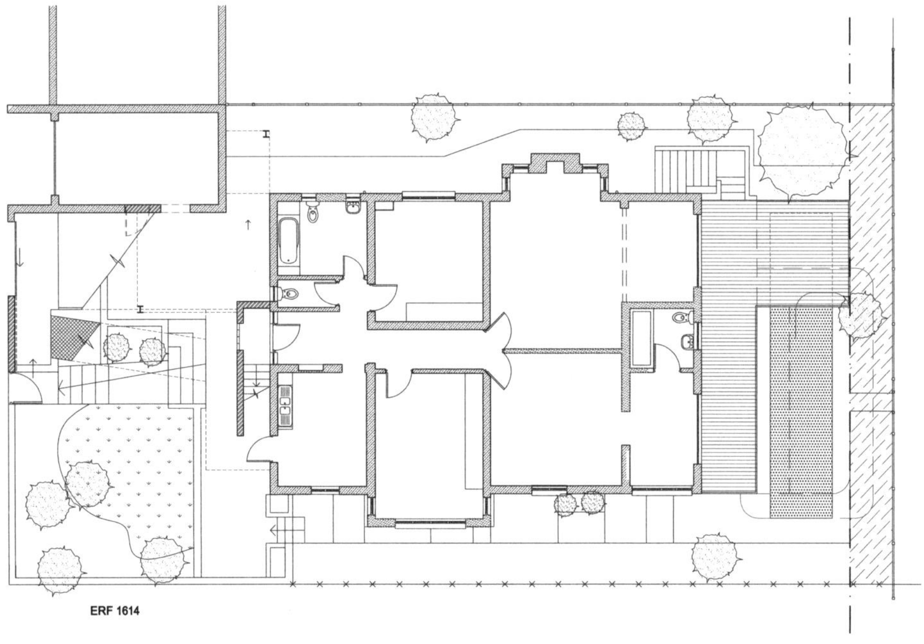

WEIRD ABOUT WIRE

WILLIE BESTER HOUSE AND STUDIO,
CAPE TOWN, WESTERN CAPE, 1996, CS STUDIO ARCHITECTS
/////////

CA245550
PRIVAAT EIENDOM
PRIVATE PROPERTY
NGUMHLABA WOMNTU LO
20

Willie Bester, born in 1956, is a pure product of the generation that paid the heaviest price for the policy of racial segregation. As a child he had to comply with the displacements under the Group Areas Act,[1] had to wait to develop his artistic expression until after his military service and then be released from a detention camp for unemployed black youth.

By Western standards, the mode of expression Bester—who trained as a dental technician—employs puts him in the field of machine manufacturing artists such as Jean Tinguely from Switzerland. He explicitly claims to be holding an art of resistance: "We must resist all that offends the human psyche; I believe we must protest against what is wrong. There is no escape; to remain apolitical is a luxury that South Africans simply cannot afford."[2] Since 1982 Willie Bester has exhibited in Africa, Europe and North America.

1
One of the pillars of the apartheid policy, issued 27 April 1950.

2
"Willie Bester", Contemporary African Art Collection by Jean Pigozzi: http://www.caacart.com/pigozzi-artist.php?i=Bester-Willie&bio=en&m=37

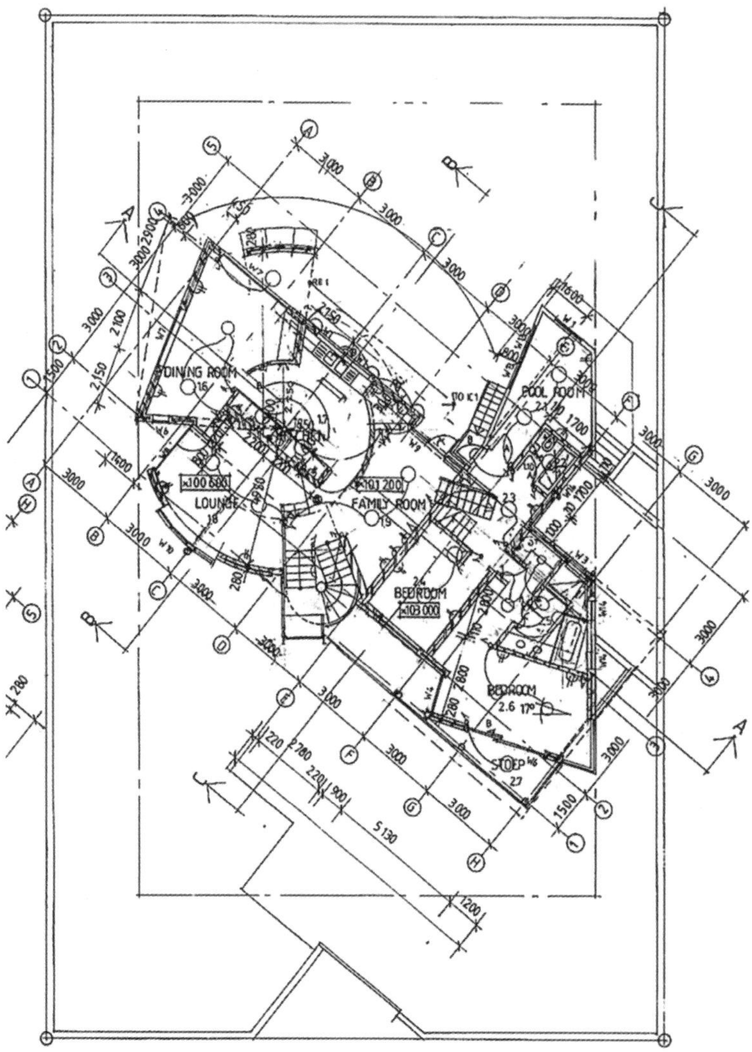

P
EXCEPT
SUNDAYS
BEHALWE.
SONDAE
TAXI
NO
DUMPING
ROME

It is with this distinguished aptitude that in 1996 Willie Bester approached the CS Studio architects, asking them to build him a house that would be a private residence, a workshop and a place for exhibition. Obviously he had defined the specifications by means of a drawing and a model made of metallic elements. Clearly, this kind of commissioning shatters the neat theoretical division taught in formal education, which defines the roles of the architect and the project owner, whereas the role of the hands becomes difficult to identify. Carin Smuts often quotes the Afro-American writer Ngugi wa Thiongo: "Culture is the product of the history of peoples; it reflects it by integrating a set of values that define their representation in space and time."

In fact the site of Bester's house/studio has drawn the attention of architects. The activity of the client and the arrangement of spaces, forms and expression were all extensively discussed among architects and generated a rich reflection on the kind of suburban detached houses that are usually meant to express the level and nature of their owners' consumer desires. The Bester house/studio gives expression to the preponderant place of the "thinking hand", dear to Juhani Pallasmaa[3] whom Carin Smuts loves to refer to. Of course, such a process is also likely to lead the architect to despair, in the sense that it can never be considered finished.

4
Juhanni Pallasmaa, *The Thinking Hand Existential and Embodied Wisdom in Architecture*, Chichester: Wiley, 2009.

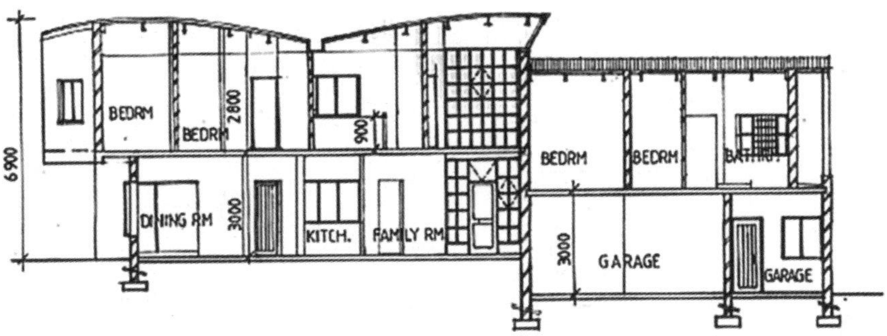

SECTION A:A

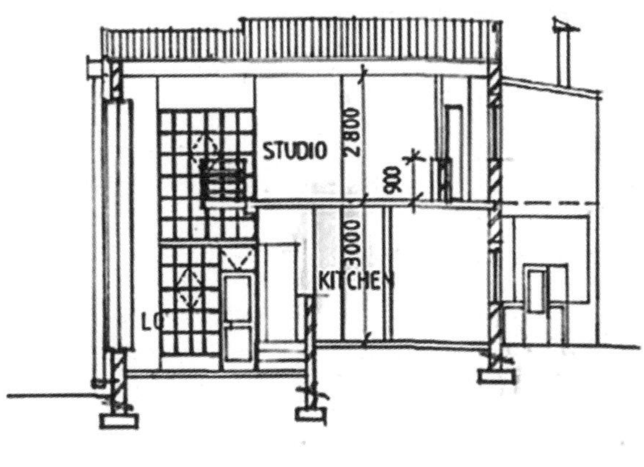

When contacted by the management of the Robben Island Trust, an organization composed of ex-prisoners responsible for development of the island and soon joined by Sheryl Ozinsky, head of Cape Town Tourism and initiator of the province's major tourist development, CS Studio Architects was supposed to project a building complex including hotels and a casino, capable of monetizing a site that offers wonderful views over Cape Town bay and on Table Mountain. The idea of the sponsors reflected the neo-Victorian vision as deployed on the other side of the bay in a lucrative waterfront. They even organized an architectural competition for the realization of this programme.

CS Studio Architects set up discussion workshops with site guides, former prisoners on the island, while at the same time the University of Cape Town, with a high concentration of leftist elements, organized a big seminar with more than 2,000 participants in which Carin Smuts had the opportunity to explain the historical and memorial value of the island where Mandela and many of his comrades were once detained. The option proposed by the architect was to build nothing at all, to proceed with the restoration of the existing buildings, and to equip them with the necessary infrastructure for receiving visitors. On the initiative of CS Studio Architects, a model of the island 2 x 2 metres, was built and installed for the information of the blind, elegantly and firmly silencing the greedy calls of "developers".

DEVELOPMENT PROJECTS, ROBBEN ISLAND [NOT A] WATERFRONT, WESTERN CAPE, 1996–1999, CS STUDIO ARCHITECTS ////////

In 1994 the first free elections took place in South Africa. They sanctioned the equality of basic civil rights and brought the ANC to power. From 1980 to 2015 the population increased sharply, from 30 to 55 million, but since 1994 the distribution of wealth has not altered. It remains highly unequal and has even worsened; the whites are the vast majority[1] of the upper 10%. Land ownership, of key importance to the field of architecture, is still affected by the segregation policies practised from 1913 to 1990 (Native Land Act); it has not been the subject of radical reform. Of all the effects of racist politics conducted by whites in South Africa, undoubtedly expropriation, deportation and population transfer had the most cruel and persistent consequences.

The Broad-Based Black Economic Empowerment (BBBEE) is a modest code of good practice intended to promote "black businesses", either owned by small, medium or very small enterprises or in the hands of black entrepreneurs. This proactive regulation, based on a quota system, was introduced in the 1990s and regularly applied since. The last revision took effect in May 2015.

Although part of a laudable intention, this regulation has many negative effects on the awarding of contracts and company shares. In practice it leads to inequality. CS Studio Architects founded Equity Studio in order to comply with this code and to have access to certain markets. The ancient ties between Carin Smuts and black communities enabled CS Studio Architects to partner with Sipho Puwane, Clint Abrahams and Vuyiswa Lamfiti. In 2016 this represents ten years of architectural practice by an architectural master. The agency therefore has a high BBBEE rating, which gives it access to public commissions.

If the cooperation of CS Studio Architects and Equity Studio is productive, it is due to the old commitment to the black communities, contrary to the policy of apartheid. In the daily management and in public works in particular, one quickly learns that things are not always easy and that this regulation can sometimes give much power to individuals who may not have adequate skills, especially as this policy develops in an environment disrupted by the corruption of political circles.

1
Thomas Piketty, "Le capital en Afrique du Sud", *Libération*, 6 October 2015.

2
CS Studio has established the Equity Studio agency to respond positively to the basic intention of the program, but it ended that experiment on 1 June 2016 due to bureaucratic mistakes and corruption problems related to its implementation.

http://simplybiz.co.za/resource-center/run-your-business/blog%252Cdocument/understanding-and-gaining-bbbee-codes.

BROAD-BASED BLACK ECONOMIC EMPOWERMENT (BBBEE)[2]

//////

Reuse: this unique term is used to describe the whole range of possible practices, whether to reinstall a building element according its initial use value, a related value or a completely new value. Niklaus Kohler[1] presents a descriptive range of levels and effects:

Reuse

Level 1	continue to use the item in its place.
Level 2	continue to use the item in a different situation, but with the same function.
Level 3	use the item in another situation and for another function.
Level 4	change the shape (the state of the material) for another use, for example, reducing a concrete element to its basic components (sand/gravel and cement) and reuse the sand/gravel for new concrete.
Level 5	discharge, dissolution, decomposition, combustion.

Balance

Level 1	recovery of energy and materials, and keeping much of the information.
Level 2	loss of much of the information.
Level 3	loss of materials, energy and information, but parts of it can be reconstructed (at the price of considerable efforts).
Level 4	down-cycling, losing everything forever—part of the energy may optionally be recovered (burning wood).
Level 5	dumping in a landfill.

1
Niklaus Kohler is professor emeritus at the Karlsruhe Institute of Technology/University of Karlsruhe and author of numerous publications on Bauforschung (literally research in the field of construction). In a recent exchange of ideas he presented us his subdivision into five levels, linked with five corresponding balance levels. We thank him warmly for his encouragement, incentive and criticism.

A SHORT VOCABULARY TO BREAK TAUTOLOGICAL LOOPS

//////

Entropy is a concept both abused and neglected. The second law of thermodynamics states that energy degrades. The energy of a complex system passes inevitably and spontaneously from concentrated forms to diffuse forms. If one admits that a building or one of its components concentrates a certain amount of energy at its origin, this energy will disperse gradually. This means that in practice, each element has the tendency to ruin and that this process will only end once the atoms of the last molecule are scattered. The potential reuse of an item cannot escape the need to assess its intrinsic level of degradation. Entropy is the definitely invincible opponent of reuse; in the whole of the process, it is responsible for rejection.

Obsolescence, by contrast, is a great ally of reuse. An object that, according to the Latin etymology, is literally "past usage and fashion", is a "high potential". Obsolescence even generates a "second market"[1] if we understand the flowering of vintage stores as a derivative of the idea of reuse, a positive symptom, synonymous with resistance to the tidal wave of the reign of commodity and its ever rolling forward. "[The] inanimate object ... clings to our soul and the power of love."[2]

The property of ***fungibility*** is a legal concept referring to the divisibility and ownership of part of a commodity or property and to substitute it for any other part thereof. Rice is a fungible commodity par excellence. We can use any isolated kilo for the same purpose as any of the other ninety-nine kilos, whereas a third of an aeroplane has very little chance of flying as only the whole is a specific and functional thing. The potential reuse of building elements is constantly confronted with this notion. It can take advantage of it, deal with it, or develop strategies to obviate the low fungibility of this or that object. This concept highlights the borderline between what can be reused and what should be rejected. It is also closely linked to the available quantity of each item.

Use value/exchange value: this basic concept is fundamental and what is more, of disconcerting simplicity as it is based on common sense. Marx largely developed its interest and scope, whereas it was already explicitly present in the writings of Aristotle. All things taken into account, reuse strategies are feasible when the object is at the intersection of the two values. In order to become suitable for construction, a building element must meet two conditions. First, its entropy should not have advanced too much, as it should have a considerable residual use value; secondly, its exchange value must be so low that there will be no buyer for it in a market. Reuse elements, marked by their non-market and non-monetary (or very limited-monetary) use value, are produced privately, for oneself, one's family, or a group to which one belongs by bonds other than those of merchants.

2
Alphonse de Lamartine, "Milly ou la terre natale", *Harmonies poétiques et religieuses*, in *Œuvres complètes*, vol. 2, Paris: Charles Gosselin, Furne et Pagnerre, 1847, 159.

They have a status similar to elements provided by nature.[3] In contrast, the market for materials that are recuperated from collected "waste" and reprocessed, or *un-cycled* to be precise (like down-cycling), and thus to be considered as ore, is developing bit by bit. And it is booming. Prices in this market reflect both its availability and the labour induced by the collecting. External factors of this process are hardly taken into account.

Intensity (quantity and quality) of the necessary work (labour expensive/labour saving): the labour intensity required for the mobilization and implementation of reusable elements is another key element of the process. It determines lastly the possibility to enter an element in the reuse cycle. It affects both the qualification and the quantity of the work. This is where the various expressions of people's creative capacities convene. At the same time, it is the human factor that links re-use with the vernacular domain and with the grey or parallel economies that thrive in neglected parts of the global market for construction materials. At this stage of the process, the engineer or architect must put their ego aside in order to enter the community of the "factory" and collegially assume the role of master builder, to share and transfer the knowledge to which they were initiated, and offer the added value of their talent. It is at this level that processes of learning, of solidarity and mutual support, of exchange of knowledge and expertise, are set up. Like *The Thinking Hand*,[4] the book *The Craftsman*[5] aggregates to a craft in which the builder recognizes and builds his or her self. It is also at this human scale that the consequences of the conflict in the field of waste recovery will come to light.

By extending its "enclaves" in the field of urban waste, contemporary capitalism, not satisfied with keeping humanity and agriculture thirsty by extending its control over privatized drinking water, nor with starving them under the pretext of feeding by submitting life to its patents and promoting grabbing of arable land, will expand its empire on the waste stemming from the incompetence of its expensive production-frenzy itself. It thus finds material for new production as well as direct and indirect prospects for new profits.

3
For this part of my reflections I owe much to Jean-Marie Harribey, "Richesse et valeur dans une perspective de soutenabilité", *ContreTemps* 4, May 2002: 71–84.

4
Juhani Pallasmaa, *The Thinking Hand Existential and Embodied Wisdom in Architecture*, Chichester: Wiley, 2009.

5
Richard Sennett, *The Craftsman*, London: Allen Lane, 2008.

This book would not have been possible without the patient availability of CS Studio, the trust and time given to me by Carin Smuts and Urs Schmid, the support and encouragement I received from Patrick Bouchain and Marie-Hélène Contal, the trust of my editor whose activism drives this publication.

I'm grateful to Philippe Loup, a true choreographer of this material who made the density of the arguments and the power of images find their respective places, to the architect Sytse de Maat, friend and translator of the English version, as well as François Hauter for his oblique view that is so welcome on a work focusing on an ultimately narrow discipline, but determined by the institutional and political context.

Project: Pierre Frey, Art Historian,
EPFL Honorary Prof., www.epfl.ch

Texts: Pierre Frey
Translation: Sytse de Maat

Quotations:

pp. 5 and 8: J. M. Coetzee. 2009. *Summertime: Scenes from Provincial Life.* London: Harvill Secker.

p. 103: J. M. Coetzee. 1998. *Boyhood: Scenes from Provincial Life.* London: Vintage

p. 109: J. M. Coetzee. 1990. *Age of Iron.* London: Secker & Warburg.

p. 169: J. M. Coetzee. 1984. *Life and Times of Michael K.* New York: Viking Press.

All images belong to CS Studio Architects, except for photography by: Amos Gitai (pp. 37, 38); Equity Studio (Pty) Ltd (pp. 84–85, 87, 88, 89, 145, 146, 148–149, 150, 152, 153, 183); Pierre Frey (pp. 43, 44, 56, 64, 72–73, 80–81, 82, 86, 96–97, 140–141, 142, 144, 147, 161, 162–163, 172–173, 174, 180–181, 182); Robert Lemermeyer (pp. 1, 2–3, 4, 9, 12–13, 23, 29, 32, 46, 68, 71, 90–91, 92, 136, 164, 184–185, 187, 190–191, 192, 195, 199, 200).

Artwork: Loup Design,
Philippe Loup, Switzerland

Editorial coordination:
Émeline Lacombe
Production:
Laurence Gibert
Copy editor:
Bronwyn Mahoney

Photoengraving:
Terre Neuve (Arles)

Printed in Portugal,
in August 2016,
by Printer Portuguesa
for Actes Sud, le Méjan,
place Nina-Berberova,
13200 Arles

ACKNOWLEDGEMENTS
//////